PHOBIAS

A COLLECTION OF TRUE STORIES

By Kay Brooks, Craig Cook, Geoffery Crescent, Kim Curley, Alyn Day, Denise Dumars, J.T. Evans, Shauna Klein, Shauna P. Norman, Angie Orenstein, David Price, Emerian Rich, Suzanne Robb, Janet Scott-Buckley, Jay Sutter, Toianna Wika

HTP

Hidden Thoughts Press

Phobias: A Collection of True Stories

Copyright © 2014 Kay Brooks, Craig Cook, Geoffery Crescent, Kim Curley, Alyn Day, Denise Dumars, J.T. Evans, Shauna Klein, Shauna P. Norman, Angie Orenstein, David Price, Emerian Rich, Suzanne Robb, Janet Scott-Buckley, Jay Sutter, Toianna Wika

First Edition

ISBN 13: 978-0615949857
ISBN 10: 0615949851

Editor: Mary Harris
Cover: Pixellogic Studio / Joseph Sigillo
Cover Photo: Lorraine Kappus Correira
Layout: The Deliberate Page / Tamara Cribley

Printed in the United States

First Printing: January, 2014

1 2 3 4 5 6 7 8 9 10

HTP

www.HiddenThoughtsPress.com

TABLE OF CONTENTS

INTRODUCTION

Phobia: from *phóbos,* meaning "fear" or "morbid fear." These fears used to be labeled "abnormal," inexplicable," or "irrational." Today, phobias are more clearly understood as a type of anxiety disorder presenting as a persistent fear of an object or a situation, and not condemned as a weakness. There are specific phobias, such as arachnophobia or fear of spiders, and there are social phobias, such as agoraphobia, or fear of going outside one's home. There are studies that show evolutionary, neurobiological, epidemiological, and/or environmental causes for phobias, which mean that there are explicit and rational reasons for individuals' fears and reactions.

What does this mean to the average person? Especially one who has a phobia, or one who loves a person who has a phobia?

Absolutely nothing.

Almost everyone is afraid of something. Given the pressures of life today, that's no surprise. And is your fear less important than my fear, because you're afraid of bacteria and I'm afraid of very large dogs? No. What's important is how we live each day to the fullest, and how we support each other in a difficult, scary, and sometimes random world.

The stories that follow show how eighteen authors discovered, and courageously live with, their phobias. I hope you find them as encouraging as I have.

Mary Harris
Executive Editor,
Hidden Thoughts Press

DOG-O-TEETH-O-PHOBIA

Jay Sutter

Two major phobias have haunted me my entire life—a fear of animals, with a major concentration in dogs and other animals that are loud or have teeth, and a social phobia, which is primarily a fear of meeting anyone new outside my small world of Jay. I do have a side effect of fearing police, but I will save discussing that phobia for another time. The dog and the social phobias are intertwined and you will see how by the end of this essay.

Between the ages of four and ten, I was painfully shy. I remember one Thanksgiving, my own grandma asked me if I wanted a bowl of ice cream. I did not answer her.

In her sweetest tone, Grandma Brown asked me again, "Jay, I know you like vanilla ice cream. Would you like some?"

I shook my head *no.*

"Jay, I know you want some. It's okay to say yes. Ice cream in a bowl?"

I shook my head *no.*

Finally, Grandma bent low, using her sweetest voice, "Jay. Have some ice cream. Will you say yes?"

Slowly, I nodded my head, indicating *yes.*

Two years prior, when Grandma Brown lived in the old white farmhouse, she owned a dachshund that chased me around her house. The more I ran, the more that demon dog nipped at me. The more I screamed, the more that monster barked and snapped at me, chasing me up the stairs. No one saved me from that high-pitched thing.

The state took Grandma's farmhouse by eminent domain to build the Mass Pike and I-91. When I was about five years old, she built a small, one level home on the same property. Grandma had a new, nicer dog, one that did not show her teeth, one that did not chase me. The dog was a basset hound ironically named Spooky. She did not bark; she howled in a grave tone. I was still afraid of her, but less so than any other dog. I kept my distance from all animals, and I never petted Spooky.

During this time, my parents took their five kids to Forest Park to see the animals. I remember going into the petting pen with what seemed like hundreds of thousands of sheep and goats. The sheep were not so scary, except for their sheer size. The goats, on the other hand, began attacking me with their teeth. They were loud and awful. Their horns scared the hell out of me, and I didn't know the word "hell" yet. The goats surrounded me, ambushing me, biting at my shirt, gnawing on my pants. I was smaller than all of them were, and I screamed and cried for help. I blanked out. I don't remember how I was rescued. Maybe my negligent father picked me up and yelled, "What'sa maaaaatta widja?" in his reminiscent growl.

I was seven years old, and in the woods with my friend, Michael Dunphy. His father's face was always red and he yelled a lot. He scared me. Anyway, Mike had a bow and arrow in the woods. He said, "Watch this." I innocently watched as Mike aimed at a frog. The arrow flew into the amphibian's middle.

The frog began hopping away with an arrow stuck in him. I was mortified. I couldn't speak or move. Although I would never touch a frog, or even go near a frog, I felt very sad about the amphibian. I saw Mike as a very mean boy. I was alarmed at this situation. Mike saw my reaction. He took the arrow out, carried the frog to the nearby house, and flung the frog over the roof. I was crushed.

When I was nine years old, a Collie chased me down Lincoln Street. The dog bit me on my arm and would not let go. I was on my way to my second-grade teacher's house. She reminded me of my grandma. Mrs. Hale usually gave me chocolate chip cookies. This beast ruined my chance to see my sweet teacher. This Collie petrified me. I screamed all the way home. When I got home, my mother checked my arm. I was not bleeding.

Growing up, we had cats. I never petted the cats, although I did enjoy playing with the cats using a chain or with catnip. I could appreciate animals from afar, but never in proximity.

I read that people with phobias tend to deal with the fear by avoidance. However, by avoidance, the fear actually intensifies. No one ever worked with me to help me "get over" my apparently irrational fears. One website stated that about twelve per cent of all Americans had a phobia, which is the "most common mental illness." What? Mental illness? It sounded so serious. I was always "different" from others.

By the time high school rolled around, I kept a pattern of walking to school, speaking to no one. I did not raise my hand. I had no friends at school. I was very athletic, yet due to my social phobias and my disdain for rules and fear of referees, I did not play organized sports. My world was after school, playing all kinds of sports with my brothers and the neighborhood kids.

During my teenage years, I was successful at avoiding meeting new people and animals, especially those with teeth. There were exceptional animals that I preferred, such as small birds that had small mouths, or beaks, although the beaks did concern me, as they are pointed. The larger birds were scarier, especially the crows, blue jays, and chickens. Chickens scared the hell out of me. They looked like dinosaurs and they were fast.

Once, I saw a friend pick up a garter snake. He called it a "gardener snake." It freaked me out that he actually touched this abnormal, crawling thing.

When I was twelve years old, I was stung by a bee. I vowed to kill every bee that summer. I used a rubber band to kill over 500 bees by September.

Horses were beautiful, but their size scared me. I rode one of those old horses when I was sixteen. I was with the neighborhood gang, so the peer pressure existed. The horse knew the trail, did not bite me, and seemed very calm. The horse walked slowly, but I did not really enjoy being on the back of a creature. I preferred to watch animals, to marvel at their beauty or at their skill.

As far as the social phobia, I didn't realize I had one until last year. I just thought that I was weird. The signs were all there my whole life. I was born backwards, tongue-tied, over half deaf, and somewhat blind. I think maybe these disadvantages affected my ability to socialize later in life. My tactile abilities are paramount, even now. I am able to read people, actually feel people's "vibes."

In a crowded room, I feel each and every person's vibe, and it is overwhelming at times, especially if the emotions are extreme. I believe that is why I have trouble being in a room with a lot of people, especially people whom I don't or can't trust.

Maybe that's why I fear cops. They tend to have that authoritarian attitude. I have trouble trusting cops. Especially K-9 cops. When I was young, I spent all my time with my three brothers and one sister and my mom. My father, when I saw him, was often drunk and loud and obnoxious. He apparently would attack my mom, but I believe I blanked almost all of that part out. I do remember on one occasion, when I was seven years old, that I stepped in between my mom and him. I faced him like a good little soldier, silently looking at him, with my mother behind me. My father turned away. I don't think he ever hurt her again. I was always small and wiry. The neighborhood boys would pick fights with me, thinking I was easy pickings. I don't know where it came from, but my shrilling war cry kicked in. I would attack the other boy at a high rate of speed. My arms would be flailing overhand like tornado-forced windmill blades with small but accurate, fleshy ball bearings pounding atop the challenger's head and face. I never lost a fight. But I never started one either, mainly because I was socially inept.

I went to the Junior High prom with Mary Sackiewicz, a beautiful cheerleader. I had no idea how to interact with her. She and I won the fast dance contest though, as it was free form, and I didn't have to stay in a box, like the playing field box, or the square classroom box, or the any other perceived social box. *"Everybody's doin' it, a brand new dance now, Come on and do the Locomotion with me."* After the prom, a half-dozen couples went to one boy's parents' house in the center of town. Some boys and girls did sexual things with one another. I just hugged Mary that night. She broke up with me the next day. I guess I was a little behind everyone else, socially and sexually.

When I was married, with three young children, the only animals we had were hamsters, cats, and a bunny. My children would want me to hold the animals, but I never felt comfortable getting that close. I wasn't really afraid of the bunny, since it seemed tame and was quiet. I just sensed that animals were not the same as people, as if I lived in a different world than they did.

I barely related to people, never mind animals. In all my jobs and wherever we lived, I was always able to avoid close proximity to animals. I could pet an old dog, as they are less menacing, but not younger ones.

Later on, I got a job as a letter carrier, delivering mail in Springfield, Massachusetts. I was a little hesitant about going door to door, as people own dogs, especially in the urban areas.

The dogs they own are often pit bulls, known for their strong jaws and sometimes violent temperament. To me, they are the *Jaws* of the city landscape. I also was concerned about my poor short-term memory adversely affecting my job performance. I have a spiritual faith that tells me to do something, even if I am afraid, and that God will help me. This would be quite a test.

The job itself was wonderful. I was outside in all kinds of weather, alone, without supervision. After about four months on the job, I had to deliver mail to a flower shop in West Springfield. As I entered, a tan Chow jumped at me. I froze. The owner of the shop said, "This is Lucy, she won't hurt you. She just wants to play." I slowly handed the owner the letters, backed up toward the door, turned, and began walking out. All the while, I was very nervous inside, with the feeling of someone watching you in the woods, waiting to pounce on you. That monster dog lunged and bit the back of my right ankle as I was almost free from that flower shop cage. I slammed the outer door and briskly walked to my truck, limping.

I called my boss, who asked if I was bleeding. I looked, and no, I was not bleeding.

He said don't worry about it and that I could fill out a form when I returned to the station. I was mortified. I was just attacked by a wild animal.

The work became quite arduous, but satisfying. There were twelve-hour days and I was paid well for my hard work. One time, I was delivering on Smith Street in Springfield. The protocol for entering a gated yard was to shake the gate before entering. If a dog came to the gate inside the yard, it was at the letter carrier's discretion whether he would proceed into that yard. I shook the gate. I entered the yard.

Suddenly, a pit bull jumped directly at me from an open front door. I faced the dog, and quickly back stepped out the gate. The dog was growling, baring its teeth, and lunging. I swung the gate closed as fast as I could.

Flump!

The dog's head was within inches of me. I was jittery. The gate door was closed on his neck. He was squirming, trying to chomp at me. I held the gate tight. He began to choke. His body was inside the yard, but his angry head and teeth were with me. The struggle seemed to last a half-hour, but in reality was just a half minute. I was not going to let go.

Finally, the owner of the monster called him back into the house. The dog yanked his head backward. I slowly let up on the gate, but not too much. The dog ran back into the open doorway. I was safe.

On another street in the same neighborhood, there was a large, old, pit bull. The owner said, "Don't worry, he has no teeth, He's old." This dog would chase me and growl at me. I took no chances. I sprayed pepper spray in front of him. I avoided delivering to that entire street if the toothless dog was loose. In fact, my personal rule was that if a dog were loose on any street, I refused to deliver mail to anyone. All owners would claim that their dog does not bite.

Wrong.

One time, a Chihuahua chased me to my truck. I sprayed him square in the nose. The dog shook its head and began walking away. Then a man came and grabbed the dog. The man began cursing me and saying, "You sprayed my dog! I'm gonna punch you out."

I was sitting in my truck, in the driver's seat. The man came up close to my window and continued to threaten me. I pointed my pepper spray nozzle at him. "Do you want to get sprayed too?"

The man punched my window and I drove off.

I often felt that I should be issued a revolver to deal with the dogs. That is how fearful I was of dogs, especially the bigger ones. Sometimes, I would pick up a large stick and carry it with me as I delivered the mail.

The last mailman story concerning dogs was the one on Sterns Street. The house was located at the end of a dead end. A five-foot chain-link fence kept the crazy jumping German Shepherd prisoner contained. This dog would jump close to the top of this fence each and every time I delivered to the mailbox located near the front door. The dog's name was Astro. One August day, I noticed that Astro was quiet. I figured he was in the back yard, maybe gnawing on a bone.

I went up the stairs to the mailbox, and placed the mail where it belonged. Suddenly, Astro's face and teeth were close to me. He was behind the screen door, trying to break through, barking extremely loudly. I quickly walked down the stairs, speed walking to my truck. As I was within twenty feet of my sanctuary, I heard the frickin' dog within striking distance. He lunged at me as I spun around in one continuous movement and swung my right arm downward and towards his biting face. Astro retreated, but kept on barking. I was full of adrenaline, scared, mad, sweating, panicky. I opened the truck door and sat in the seat, slumping. I breathed a sigh of relief. The owners came outside, retrieved Astro, and asked me if I was okay. I said that I thought I was all right. The owners went inside.

I felt some pain, so I looked down. My shorts were bloody. That evil monster bit my testicles and penis. I told the owners. They offered me a Band-Aid.

I called my boss. He asked me why I didn't follow the safety procedures! What?

I drove to the hospital and the nurse immediately gave me a tetanus shot. She then said that she was going to give me Novocain where I was bitten, followed by stitches. I said no. We'll just let it heal naturally. No way was I going to get a painful shot down there! The nurse cleaned me up and bandaged me the best she could. I returned to work the next day. Everyone treated me like a hero, and gave me the superhero name Iron-Balls.

There were many, many other instances of near bites and fearful situations concerning dogs, but the strangest animal encounter I had was with a couple of chickens.

It was while I was delivering on Pine Street. It was a beautiful spring day. As I approached a house dedicated to helping alcoholics and drug users, I saw them. One was black, the other was white. They were walking toward me. Two large chickens. I backed up and retreated to my truck. I called the supervisor. The chickens stayed in front of the house, baiting me to approach. I told my supervisor, "There are two cocks on Pine Street, one white and one black. They won't let me deliver the mail." I figured that if I used humor, then it would lighten the situation. The supervisor laughed. I explained it.

He said he would send out Animal Control to pick the cocks up. They never showed up and I skipped that part of Pine Street that day.

Another time, there was a rogue turkey in the Sunset Street area. The darn turkey ran straight at my truck as I was traveling at 35 mph. He was trying to commit suicide. Who would have figured? It was Thanksgiving time, though. This is a true story. But I was not afraid of him, since I was in my truck. I had to stop and wait for the turkey to walk away. That wild turkey beat me at the game of chicken.

Later, there were two dogs that helped me to manage my perceptions and fears of them. First was Nikki. She was my second wife's cattle dog. She was a bit pingy, bouncing here and there. But she never bit nor bared her teeth. She loved to play with balls and Frisbees. I loved her "mommy," so it was easier to love Nikki. Eventually, Nikki developed an inoperable tumor. She also had degenerative arthritis and lost the use of her back legs. We took her to be euthanized. My wife held her dying dog. I petted Nikki. I remained silent and meditative. I realized that I loved Nikki, even if she was a dog.

A few months later, my wife was dog-sitting a Rhodesian Ridgeback named Homer. The owner saw how much she loved Homer and let Homer stay for good.

Homer was a loud barker. He would bark at everything: a passing car, the leaves blowing in the wind, coyotes. I warmed up to him in time, although the volume of his voice was unnerving. Homer was a smart dog. He knew German commands, like

Platz—lie down, and *Steh*—stand. He traveled in the front seat with me. I took him for long walks. He would lay by the wood stove as I loaded it with ash that I split. Now, I am separated from him, not by choice. I have his picture as my cellphone screensaver. Boy, do I miss Homer.

I am still afraid of dogs. I freeze when a dog is in my proximity. Usually, the dog will nip at me or jump on me or bump me to show dominance. I submit. My daughter and her boyfriend opened up a tattoo parlor in New Orleans recently. They also bought a large house nearby. My son moved down and lives in the apartment that is attached to the tattoo parlor. This past year, I went to visit.

Problem was, there were three dogs living in the large house, two Bulldogs and one foxhound. There were two other dogs in the tattoo parlor apartment, a nervous mutt and a small terrier. Here we go again, into the jaws of danger.

My first day in the big house was interesting. The bulldog, named Jughead, looked like a clown; his face was goofy and he was clumsy. He liked me immediately. Jughead slobbered his saliva all over my shirt and pants. I liked his demeanor, but I really did not want to be kissed or licked in the face. I was very uncomfortable, but wanted not to offend my daughter, so I sucked it up. The dogs must have sensed that my daughter loved me, and I, her.

The other bulldog, named Dude, was only a year old and already very obstinate and cranky. He did accept me, but would try to do the dominance thing on me. I was truly scared, but again, tried to be strong. I could pet both these dogs, but did not want licks.

The third dog was named Chicken (haha!). She was an older dog who mediated between the bulldogs. She was the queen, barking and baring her teeth. Wow, she was sweet to humans, but serious with dogs.

One day, my daughter and her boyfriend noticed a lady down the street dragging a small puppy using a bed sheet wrapped around the poor thing's neck. My daughter's boyfriend offered to buy the puppy from her for $40. She agreed. This puppy was a beautiful Australian Cattle Dog, or Blue Heeler, similar to Nikki, the sweet dog who died in my presence. They named the pup Ruby. This dog was smart, and fast, and oh so cute. But, she would bite ankles, as she was genetically conditioned to do. I would raise my legs up and keep her from me. I was secretly afraid of her bites.

As I was the only one in the apartment during the day, I would make it my job to watch the three dogs, Whatusi the mutt, Barnum the terrier, and Ruby. It was like juggling. Barnum would hump Whatusi, and Ruby would bite Whatusi. Then Whatusi would break out in nervous hives.

Barnum got his name from the Barnum & Bailey Circus. That is, Barnum would perform a trick when he wanted a treat. He would stand up on his hind legs, then twirl around and around. He could turn perpetually if the treat was held above him.

Whatusi was the most patient dog I ever experienced. I imagine it was because she was previously abused prior to being rescued from the shelter. It made me realize that dogs each have personalities like we humans do. I spent about thirty hours per week with the three dogs, and I gained a greater confidence to be with them, to appreciate them, and eventually, to love them. By taking care of the dogs, I overcame some of my fears. I actually miss the dogs to this day and look forward to seeing them again.

Recently, I had a lot of trouble adapting to the bully bosses in the post office. I spent ten years in the Air Force and never had a problem working hard or having respect for my superiors. Every command and order the military officers gave me made sense, and the room to perform was not questioned. When I became a letter carrier, the bosses attempted to beat down every employee emotionally, to ensure that the workers were compliant and afraid. It did not work with me.

I tried to reason with the bosses. They got worse. I tried to raise my voice to meet theirs. They got worse. I tried to remain silent. They got worse.

I was fired about eight times in eight years. Each and every time, I received my job back, as the union fought for me, and I stood strong. Eventually, I went to therapy, and I found that I had Asperger's Syndrome. This explained to me why I had social issues, and why I had difficulty with my bosses. It also shed light on why I had a phobia about animals, particularly with dogs. People in this autistic spectrum tend to deal better with inanimate objects, such as machinery or computers. Interacting with living things is more difficult.

With this in mind, I realized that I was born with this syndrome, so my fear of certain social situations and my phobias are firstly hereditary in nature. I submit this as a possible theory for all phobias. Could it be that certain people have a genetic predisposition to fear? It is entirely plausible. Of course, nature can influence the phobias, too. Dogs instinctively sense when a person is afraid. The dog's reaction to a person with a fear of dogs can further increase that fear, thus ensuring the dog's show of dominance over the individual.

With this information, I try to steel myself, to relax, to breathe deeply. I try to trick myself into being confident when meeting a new dog. I will place my hand low in an upward cupped position, as those in dog circles have instructed, to show friendship. I am still afraid of dogs, but I have come a long way in loving them. My daughter told me that I should have a dog of my own.

Maybe I will.

DREAMING OF THE DEAD

Suzanne Robb

When I saw the blue car in the driveway, I flew out of the one I was in and ran up the walkway to the house. My grandparents were there—more importantly, my Papa. I struggled with the door until it opened with the aid of my mom from the inside.

I went straight for the kitchen, ignoring my towering grandmother. I looked all over the place, but no Papa. I glanced up at Granny and asked, "Where's Papa?"

"He's mowing the lawn," she replied as she looked at me with a tired expression.

I went to the patio door and tried to find my Papa in the nighttime darkness. My five-year-old mind did not realize cutting the grass was a day thing. As I searched, my dad came up behind me and led me into my parents' bedroom.

We sat on the side of the bed and as he stared straight ahead, he spoke. "Papa's gone, he's not coming back."

"Where did he go?" I had never experienced death before.

"Heaven. He's in Heaven now, in the clouds, because he's dead."

My father stood and left me in the room as he mingled with other family members who'd come over. I went to my room and played, not really understanding why everyone was so upset.

A month later, we took a plane down to Florida for an impromptu vacation. Since I was a hyper child, my mom thought it would be a good idea to give me the window seat. I stared out of it for hours, so much so that the stewardess who gave me my wings, something they did back in the eighties for kids, asked me what was so interesting.

"I'm looking for my Papa. My dad told me he was up in the clouds now."

The woman nodded and left. My mom told me to hush and sit back while she pinned the wings on me.

"You can't see Papa. Just because Heaven is in the clouds doesn't mean you can see him."

None of this made sense. I knew they had had a funeral, but none of the grandchildren were allowed to attend because it was a stuffy British event where everyone had a stiff upper lip and acted as if nothing had happened, which meant the gravity of what was going on around me didn't hit.

While on vacation, my parents went out one night, leaving me with the control for the television. I flipped through the channels and a movie caught my attention. The film was in black and white and the two main characters were in a graveyard when my channel surfing stopped.

I continued to watch, and remember the line, "They're coming to get you, Barbara."

I watched in horror as dead people rose from their graves, some in suits, others in rags. I realized dead people were coming back to life and eating the living. The movie was called *Night of the Living Dead* and to this day, I cannot watch it.

I had my first nightmare that night. I dreamt my Papa came back to life and his skeletal body rambled around the house trying to eat me. My parents were upset with me for watching a scary movie and told me not to do it again, it wasn't real.

From then on, at least twice a week, nightmares of dead people chasing me invaded my dreams. I would be running in a dark area, where the trees were cartoon-like and reached out to grab me. I heard heavy breathing behind me, and every time I turned to look, the thing was closer. Eventually, it would bite my shoulder and I would wake screaming, on occasion throwing up.

Other dreams involved me being in the center of a circle of zombies piled so high I could not see the top, and in order to escape, I had to climb over the rotten bodies as they tried to scratch and bite me.

My parents assumed it was a phase and left it alone. When we would drive by cemeteries, I would get goose bumps and search for any wandering zombies.

When I was seven, we were driving around the city of Chicago with some relatives when the car jerked to a halt. A second later, a man crashed into the rear window of the car, then stared at me, bloodied.

Bits of glass debris stuck out of his face, and he looked at me as he asked for help. I convinced myself he was a zombie and wanted to eat me. My mom dragged me out of the car and we stood off to the side as paramedics removed the motorcyclist from the car and worked on him.

I cried the entire time, terrified that dead people were lurking at every turn. This started another period when I woke up in the middle of the night, screaming from the nightmarish images of the dead, and was sick to my stomach.

My parents never knew what to do. Having had a child in their older years, their patience and understanding was low. Not to mention that my dad dealt with emotions by ignoring them.

During that summer, my great-uncle was diagnosed with cancer, and my mom took me to visit him in a hospice for very ill patients. When I looked into the rooms we passed, bodies were on the beds, with thin, paper-like skin, sunken faces, and mouths open for no reason. My uncle did not look much different, and the entire time, I thought it was in some sort of hospital for zombies.

The concepts of cancer and hospices were beyond me. My mom tried explaining it was a place for people who were too sick to get better and would end up in Heaven. This made me even more scared, and I realized sick or dying people either looked like zombies, or became them after they went to Heaven.

My mom never took me back, most likely because the nightmares and throwing up in the middle of the night began again.

For years, this went on, terrifying dreams about zombies. Sometimes I was bitten; other times, I escaped. On especially bad nights when I woke up, I would see shadows in my room that sent terror through me. My parents didn't comfort me, but did get upset when I was tired in the morning.

As I got older, and zombie and horror movies became more popular, my life turned into hell. I could watch vampires, werewolves, serial killers, any graphic horror movie imaginable, because it did not compare to what I dreamt about at night. Problem was, as soon as a zombie movie came on, I started to hyperventilate. I made some excuse to leave the room and wait until the movie was over. If it was a rental, I couldn't sleep until it was returned to the video store. Just having the cassette in the house was enough to keep me up at night.

While in college, I managed to avoid zombie movies, but after being diagnosed with a brain tumor, death obsessed me. I didn't realize it at the time. Then again, who would not freak out about a mass of unknown origin in their head like a ticking time bomb? My friends thought about dating or parties, and I wondered how much longer I had to live.

My doctor reassured me it was nothing major. "Slow growing," he said, "The best kind of tumor to have."

The nightmares started up again and my love of horror movies skirted around anything zombie-related. My friends thought I was being immature or foolish, but they weren't there at three in the morning, when I would be sitting next the toilet tossing my pizza.

Every noise I heard was a zombie. I realized it was irrational, but in my fear-drenched state, it made perfect sense to me. When my dad died, my mom didn't want me to take a plane home for the funeral. September 11, 2001 was still too fresh, and she told me she didn't want to risk me dying.

My nightmares turned into my dad coming after me. He screamed at me for not going to his funeral. He chased me around, his cancer-ravaged body rotten and decayed. For weeks, I slept in bursts because of the fear of sleeping.

I stopped telling people because I was tired of hearing how lame I was acting, or that I just needed to grow up.

Eventually, my mom and I moved back to Canada and I started a new round of doctors for the thing in my head. After several tests, consults, and anxiety attacks, the specialists determined that the tumor was nothing more than an anomaly, which might cause me discomfort and the occasional bit of imbalance.

I sighed with relief, but then was assigned a therapist to deal with the anxiety I developed.

After two years, she asked me about my obsession with zombies. I had no idea what she was talking about, and commented as such.

"Every time you talk about the tumor, you reference dying, or having it scramble your brains so badly you become a zombie, among other worries such as going crazy and ending up in an institution on so many drugs that you'll walk around like a zombie."

I wanted to tell her she was wrong, that she had no idea what she was talking about. But as I looked back at how I saw things, I realized dying, going crazy, medication, and everything in between were related to zombies for me.

Without telling my therapist, I saw two different hypnotherapists for a fear of flying. I missed my friends and needed to visit them. Only problem was, planes terrified me. Not because I thought it would crash, but because if I asked the captain to pull over, chances were he would say no.

The reason I went to two was because the first one was obsessed with treating me for *thanatophobia*. When I asked him what it was, he told me it was a fear of death. I laughed at him. Fear of death? I had had a brain tumor hanging over my head for almost five years before I found out it would not kill me. If that didn't get me over a fear of death, nothing would. I also pointed out I was there for flying.

He argued with me and told me my fear of death was the main issue that needed treating. I found another hypnotherapist, and he told me the same thing after two sessions. I went back to my therapist, writing off hypnotherapy as a waste of time and money.

My usual therapist was upset with me and I had no idea why. She later explained my fear of death manifested itself in a specific way, through zombies. The other therapists didn't meet with me or delve deep enough to realize that, so any therapy they did was wasted money on my part, according to her.

I asked why she didn't tell me sooner and she told me I wasn't ready to hear it. A fear so embedded, like thanatophobia, was not something she could desensitize me to, or rationalize away. Everybody dies. Most people are afraid of it. However, most people are not so scared to the point that zombies dominate their fear of having a life.

At this time, since my fear of death was revealed, she started to address it. At first, through small things, like having a zombie movie in the house. I thought it was silly, a movie in the house—easy. I remember going to the store and standing in the horror section looking for zombie movies, the covers on them enough to make me nervous.

I grabbed the first one I found, *Dawn of the Dead,* bought it, and walked around the mall feeling like people were watching me. As soon as I arrived home, I put the movie with the others and tried to forget about it.

That night I heard the steps cracking. The dog moved and scared the crap out of me, and I ended up thinking about the movie the whole time. After a week, it stopped bothering me, but the nightmares were back. I would wake up covered in sweat and glance to the door, convinced a zombie was about to pop out.

When I talked to my therapist, she explained I needed to separate the two, that zombies were not death, just a representation of my fear. She recommended I write about them, since I enjoyed writing short stories just for fun at the time.

The whole thing sounded like a waste of time to me, but I did as told. I sat down and began to write a zombie tale, stopping after ten minutes because I was so scared. Then the idea formed in my head and I wanted to finish writing it.

The end result was nothing extraordinary; rather dull, actually. My therapist recommended I continue to do small activities like watching the zombie movies, and to continue to write the short stories. She worked with me on my nightmares, teaching me how to control them.

What happened was I would watch a movie or write a story about something that scared me. The same night, I would have a nightmare about one of the two. When I tried to change the way the nightmare went, it would backfire.

Instead of turning the zombies into something harmless, or overcoming them, I would get bit as others escaped. Once they bit me, the zombies were no longer interested in me and I sat and watched as hundreds of them walked by me, as if I were one of them.

Being afraid to die is not something one easily overcomes, especially when it is linked to such a visceral image. What makes things worse is the popularity of zombies in books, short stories, movies, television shows.

I followed the advice of my therapist for two years before it finally started to work. I could control my nightmares, and watch a movie without a follow-up nightmare, or a vomit session in the bathroom. And ironically, many of the short stories I write now are about zombies. This is, of course, because every time I write a story, it brings me that much closer to ridding myself of the fear. The fact I make them humorous to some degree also aids in lessening the phobia I have.

Thanatophobia is the fear of death. For me, it manifested itself in the shape of zombies due to the combination of the death of my Papa and seeing a scary movie at a young age. For years, I dreamt of the dead coming to get me. I hid this from most people because even talking about it brought on a bout of new nightmares.

After almost 30 years, I am virtually free of the terror that watching a movie used to cause me. A healthy fear of death is normal; I know that. I will always have some sort of niggling thought of it in the back of my head, but the manifestation of zombies that used to dominate my dreams is all but gone.

I admit, some movies still scare the crap out of me, and some books I have to read in the daytime. But the nightmares have lessened to the point that they occur only about twice a year, and they are not as intense as they once were.

One day, I know they will be gone for good, and until then, I use the imagery to help my writing.

EIGHT FEET OF TERROR

Janet Scott-Buckley

It must be the legs. Eight just seems like too many. Though I believe it's more than just the legs.

Let me start over. I am not a fan of "bugs." Insects, whether they crawl, fly, or slither, are not creatures I want to get very close to. However, the six-legged types do not bother me nearly as much as their eight-legged relatives. I am terrified of spiders. You'd have to call it a phobia, since a phobia, by definition, is usually inexplicable and illogical.

I have no idea why I am so afraid of spiders. I have no early memory that would indicate some spider-related trauma that could have caused this fear. Perhaps if I were to participate in some kind of hypnotism or past-life regression therapy, I would discover a valid reason for my problem. For now, it remains unexplained, therefore, a true phobia.

I killed one this morning, which is a big step for me. Usually, I try to have someone else kill them for me. I was making the bed when suddenly something small and black ran across the bedspread. I could tell right away what it was. Don't ask me how I could tell. It's an uncanny ability that must be a part of my neurosis. I can tell the difference between a spider and say, an ant, even at a distance, and even if the thing is moving very fast. This one was moving fast.

I grabbed a box of tissues, slammed the box on top of the spider about four or five times, checking each time to see if the thing was dead, finally stopping when I was convinced it was. Then I took about three or four tissues out of the box and scooped up the corpse. I did not dispose of it in the trashcan by the bed. That would be unacceptable. I have this irrational fear that the body might reanimate somehow and come back during the night for vengeance.

As I mentioned before, I don't like other "bugs" or insects either. They all give me the creeps. I have a lot of allergies, so I was always pretty afraid of being stung by a bee, in case I had an allergic reaction. I was stung a few years ago, with little effect, so bees don't even worry me very much now.

I live in a rural neighborhood with a lot of trees and wildlife, so bugs are a part of my life now, moreso than ever before. Each year, we seem to have a different infestation. I guess bugs come and go with different weather patterns. One year, it was tiny ants; another year, it was large ants. We also are inundated with "stink bugs" most summers. Stink bugs are ugly; they really look like they've arrived from some alien planet. They are also strange in that they crawl excruciatingly slowly, with their long antennae wiggling, yet when they take off in flight, they launch themselves like a rocket with a loud buzzing sound. Somehow, these little aliens do not terrify me.

I had a job once for which I did community outreach in inner city neighborhoods. Many of the homes I visited had cockroach problems. One that I remember clearly was so infested that I had to leave all of my belongings locked in the trunk of my car, bringing only a notepad and pen, as I didn't feel comfortable putting anything on the floor or furniture that I would have to then carry into my car or, worse yet, into my home. I would sit on the edge of a chair, with only my toes touching the floor, and would have to move my feet out of the way of the roaches as they came by. Gross, yes. I hated those things. But I did not fear them the way I fear spiders.

Over the years, people have tried to rationalize to me why I should not be so afraid of spiders. "Look at Charlotte in *Charlotte's Web*," they'd say. "Now, that's a nice spider, right?"

I never liked that book, or the movie, for that matter. I did like the nursery rhyme about Little Miss Muffet. I totally related to that girl!

Spiders have featured in other forms of entertainment as well, such as TV and movies. A child of the seventies, I used to love watching *Gilligan's Island* and *The Brady Bunch*. I clearly remember some episodes of those amusing comedies that were pretty scary due to some large spiders that featured prominently in the plots.

I always loved horror movies. Give me a great story about a killer dog, a possessed car, or a serial murderer any day. I never was able to sit through an entire screening of *Arachnophobia*. Some folks have tried to explain to me how spiders are "clean" bugs, and how they eat the "bad" bugs. That hasn't helped me to overcome my problem.

The uncanny thing about my phobia is that spiders seem to be attracted to me somehow. I swear some of the situations I have found myself in would not happen to most people.

When I was about fifteen and had my first summer job, I was working evenings at a local grocery store. I remember one night coming home tired, just wanting to go to bed and get some sleep. It was a sweltering August night. The lamp near my bed had been on for a while and the bulb was hot. Apparently the heat of the bulb had acted as a kind of incubator to a mother spider's egg sac. I crawled into bed, leaned over to switch off the lamp, and was horrified to see what appeared to be thousands of miniscule spiders hanging from my lamp. One can of Raid later, I still slept in a different room that night.

I also remember a situation in my twenties when I could have been killed due to my unfounded fear. I was driving with a friend from graduate school at night, and a spider suddenly dropped from the visor just in front of my line of vision. Fortunately, I had the presence of mind to control myself long enough to pull the car safely over to the side of the road.

As is often the case when someone has a great fear of something, I have developed a high sensitivity to the presence of spiders. My eyesight is not great. I am nearsighted and wear glasses for both driving and watching movies or television. However, even without my glasses on, I can spot a spider on the ceiling from across the room. I am also short, and since spiders seem to like high places, I often cannot reach high enough to kill them. One particular fear is that in reaching to kill one that is up high, I will miss and it will land on me. Yuck.

My husband and my son have learned to react pretty quickly when I call out, "Spider!" I'm the spotter; they are the trappers and killers. I used to drive my husband crazy with my request to see proof, the corpse, before he threw the balled-up tissue in the trash. Now that my son is five-foot-seven, he has become the primary spider killer in the family. Every teenager needs chores, right?

I routinely check the walls and ceiling at night when I go to bed, before turning out the light, or even before relaxing to read a book. If I notice a dark spot that may appear to be moving, I call my son in to take a closer look. A few weeks ago, I called him in at about nine o'clock at night.

"Sean," I said, "stand on the bed and look at that black thing on the ceiling for me."

"Okay," he said, climbing up and standing on the bed. "What?"

"What is it?" I asked. "Is it a spider?"

"Mom," he answered, "it's the same dirt spot you had me look at last month, it hasn't moved."

As you can imagine, camping or any kind of "roughing it" is a bit of a challenge for me. We have good friends with a nice, rustic cottage on a lake in New Hampshire. They are kind enough to invite us up there with them, usually a couple of times each summer. I love going there. The first thing I do when I go into the bedroom is look for spiders, and I am on alert each night.

I wish that this story had a happy ending. I wish I could say that I have conquered my irrational fear. I have not. I have learned to live with it, and I am honest about it, which is probably important. I really am not embarrassed to tell people how I feel about spiders. I manage a business office, and the women in the office know that if there's a spider in the ladies' room—"One of Janet's friends," they'll laughingly call it—they need to get rid of it.

Fortunately, the people around me seem to accept my problem, and while they may tease me a bit, they seem to understand for the most part. Maybe that's because most people are afraid of something.

FAMILY, FROGS, AND PHOBIAS

Shauna Norman

Yesterday, I received this beautiful bookmark from my friend in the Upper Hunter Valley. A bookmark is a very appropriate gift for me because I read with a passion; however, I can usually have anything up to four books, and more at times, going at once. Why is one appropriate for me?

Firstly, because 'that' my friend Yvonne bought me an almost identical one a couple of years ago, as a going-away gift before I left to spend a couple of months in Melbourne.

Secondly is, of course, the very fact that they both bought bookmarks. Up until now, I don't recall ever receiving a bookmark as a gift and if I have I cannot, this moment, remember it.

Thirdly is that they are both green diamante frogs. They are different shades of green; one is much darker than the other, and the most recent is sporting a red diamante kerchief; otherwise, they would be twins.

Now, the fact that they are frogs is what really astounds and amuses me, and as you read on, you will see why.

When I was in my very early twenties, I found I had a collection of ornamental frogs—stuffed frogs, salt and pepper shaker frogs, candle frogs, big frogs, little frogs, all coloured frogs. I am sure it had started quite innocently. Someone gave me a frog, someone saw this frog and bought me another one, and somewhere down the line, people assumed I liked frogs. So, for Christmas, Easter, birthdays, and probably even just because "I like you," I received frogs instead of flowers and chocolates or more appropriate gifts.

The thing was, not only did I not like frogs—I was terrified of the creepy, slimy, green amphibians. Be that as it was, they kept on coming until I had a hundred or so of them.

This story takes on an even more bizarre twist, though; you see, my first husband was very jealous and very violent (he had his own demons to cope with) and one night, in a fit of rage, he started throwing the frogs off the second-floor balcony of the unit where we lived. He was screaming that I thought more of the frogs than I did of him.

One after another, these dust-collecting mementos flew through the air and landed in the boughs of trees, headless in the gravel, and in the mouths of local canines, which undoubtedly carried them away to rip to shreds and then possibly bury in some sacred stuffed toy graveyard.

Back to the frogs; they were finally gone. Well most of them, and my ex-husband thought he was hurting me. Truth was, I was relieved to see most of them go.

Looking back into my childhood, I have very vivid memories of a sadistically perverted uncle who, when he became aware of my phobia, would make a point of searching out and collecting the large green frogs that hung around the water tanks (anyone who has lived in rural Australia will know the ones I am referring to) and pretend he had a gift or a treat for me in his hand for me. When I cautiously ventured close enough, he would throw them on me or try to stick them down my shirt. Is there any wonder I would later require therapy?

Another example of just how scared I was of frogs comes to mind. I was living in

Grafton, in New South Wales, with my two young sons. We had been outside playing and were about to enter the house when I noticed, halfway down the hall, a massive tree frog sitting nonchalantly on the carpet. I could only access the bedrooms. The offending interloper stood between me and the rest of the house.

I sidled closely along the wall, in and out of each bedroom, and packed clothes enough for the three of us for a day or two. I then prepared the boys to travel and locked the house from the outside. With my sons on either side of me, we set off to hitchhike the thirty-odd miles to my mother's place; I didn't drive and it was much safer to hitch a ride between the small country towns back then than it is now. After filling mum in, I wasted no time finding someone who would not only drive us home again, but was also willing to remove the uninvited green boarder from our cozy little home.

Some people laughed, some berated me for being both silly and reckless, and at least one understood. I do not remember, as it was such a long time ago, who took me seriously enough to rid me of the old frog and place him back in his own habitat, but apparently, someone did. Fear is fear, no matter how it is decorated or disguised, and should be acknowledged as such.

Am I over it? There was a time, not all that long ago, when I was staying with someone in Grafton, that this was put to the test. Her generous daughter had travelled literally miles with her children to help clean out what could only be termed a disgustingly smelly overgrown section of the yard. We continually tied up bag upon bag of dog bones, pulled out the front fender of a car, a section of floor carpeting, and toys, and chipped away at grass almost up to our bottoms. Talking of bottoms, the woman who lived there repeatedly disappeared while we worked ours off.

In amongst this overgrown dumping ground, we stumbled upon the homes of myriad brown frogs, penny lizards, and garden worms. Basically, I was just fine. I was more concerned about the news shared by the next-door neighbour that she had killed two snakes in the past week.

I believe this is one fear I have overcome with the help of Emotional Release Therapy—Sandplay and Transpersonal Breathwork were two specific techniques used to address my fears.

You see, it was during therapy, i.e., a good therapist, and a strong commitment from me to be willing to delve into my psyche, that we revealed (I remembered) my sister had collected a jar of almost fully developed tadpoles from the culvert down the road and when she was about to be caught with them by a tyrannical parent, she hid the jar—tadpoles and all—way up under my bed.

Apparently, I ended up with these hopping mad creatures, in search of a mother figure, all through my bed, and thus the nightmares of a frog-leaping kind begun.

I'm not saying I would lovingly embrace a frog, but there have been times when I have been confronted with a situation that I have managed quite well. So I guess you could say I have learnt to co-exist with them, as long as they keep their distance.

A classic example was when a friend and I travelled out to the Tamworth Country Music Festival. During the evening, I went to use the ladies room. A big green tree frog had jumped through the window and was perched precariously on the back of the system near the seat. I found I had to ask my host to please remove it so that I could utilize the amenities, but my heart rate was not too bad. I checked the room each time

I entered after that; however, I was not anxious about it and let's face it, who would not have reacted in a similar manner?

Therefore, the fact that two of my friends both gave me almost identical frog bookmarks within a year or so is nothing more than a cute (and much loved and appreciated) coincidence, and more about me being a book reader—and my friends buying me very thoughtful personal gifts—than it is about me again becoming a collector of inanimate frogs.

KATSARIDAPHOBIA

Shauna Klein

Katsaridaphobia is such a long and complicated word for an equally nasty and disgusting bug, the roach. Yes, I have a fear of roaches but not just any roach; I have a phobia of what we call in the South palmetto bugs. They're huge, ugly roaches that grow up to almost two inches in length and—wait for it—they can fly.

I live in Florida, and we enjoy warm, tropical weather and stunning beaches. However, you take the good with the bad. Along with the good we also get hurricanes, we're the lightning capital of the country and yes, we get enormous roaches.

I don't remember the first time I became afraid of them, but I certainly have stories of times when I was terrified of them. I grew up in a house that was next to a neighbor who had a wooded area in his backyard. This may sound normal, but picture every other house in the neighborhood having a green lawn in the backyard. This neighbor was different, and unfortunately, palmetto bugs thrive in wooded areas, just like they love moist, warm climates. My mom kept a spotless house and when I say spotless, I mean getting down on the floor on her hands and knees to scrub the grout with a toothbrush. However, this did nothing to deter the palmetto bugs from getting into the house. It seems that they can flatten themselves until they scurry under doors and any flaws in the perimeter that give them access.

My bedroom had two doors. One led to my mom and dad's room (picture having to go through their room every time you needed to use the bathroom) and the other one led into the utility room, where there was a washer, dryer, walk-in closet, cabinets, and a deep freezer. My mom and dad also kept a big bag of dog food in there. One night, I kept hearing something scratching around. It was driving me crazy, so, like any person you see in a horror movie, I got up to investigate. I turned on the light in the utility room and when I did, two palmetto bugs came flying out of the bag of dog food and zoomed around the room. I didn't scream, but I almost passed out from fright. I quickly shut the door and ran back to my bed, as if that would keep them away from me. Remember the ability to get under doors? Well, it took care of the problem for the moment, anyway, and I imagine they went back to their meal of tasty, dried dog food.

Another time that was particularly horrifying was when my dad had gone out to move a doghouse, and when he picked it up, a hoard of the nastiest palmetto bugs you've ever seen ran out and started climbing his legs. Now, you can be the toughest person I know and dad was not afraid of them, but if you have tons of them climbing up your legs, you might freak out, too. I was screaming, he was jumping around, and then things got worse. He was in his bare feet when he accidentally kicked the cement base that the doghouse had been resting on and tore his big toenail off.

You see, if you happen to come across a palmetto bug, they run around like they don't know what they are doing. You can never tell where they are going to go, so they could very well fly onto you, run under something and hide, or anything at all—there is no rhyme or reason to what they'll do. That makes them worse, because no one can predict their next move. One minute you're heading into the kitchen for a glass of water, and the next minute a creature sent from the depths of Hell itself is running at your feet.

When I say they are evil, I mean it. I almost got into a car wreck once because one got in the car. They're very quiet unless they're clicking their feet on the floor. Otherwise, one moment you're watching television or something normal and the next, there one is, right up close to you. They're like little ninja bugs.

This one had been on the car somewhere, I imagine, and when I opened the door to get in, it ran inside. It waited until I was driving down the road, then proceeded to make an appearance. I actually ran off the road.

I was around nineteen years old and honestly, I wasn't the best driver anyway, so that didn't help things at all. I got off the highway and ran out of the car until it got out. They say that people get into wrecks quite often when a bee gets in their vehicle, but what about roaches? I'll take a bee any day over a palmetto bug.

The problem is, unless I move to a colder climate I'll always have the fear of these creatures. However, I've seen plenty of horror movies, and while they may not be called palmetto bugs up north, I've seen the huge roaches that can get into houses and restaurants, so honestly, there are not many places that I wouldn't be exposed to them, although I think Florida is one of the worst areas to find them. Just writing about them gives me the chills and makes me keep looking around to make sure one isn't nearby. They seem attracted to your thoughts. If you think of one, one shows up somehow. Remember the legend about saying "Bloody Mary" in the mirror three times and she'd show up? I think that is how palmetto bugs are; you think of one and one shows up. You don't even have to say it three times!

The odd thing is, when I was very little I was scared of spiders, not palmetto bugs. We'd go to my granddad's house and when it'd start getting dark, the spiders would come out of the cracks in the porch. He lived in an old, wooden house in the woods and these were the biggest spiders I'd ever seen—I was terrified of them at the time. Oddly, that switched to the palmetto bugs and I have no idea why.

Some people say fear or phobia is due to something that has happened to you, but I can't recall any particular moment when something happened that frightened me involving a palmetto bug. It's like one day I was just scared of them, and that hasn't changed in more than 25 years.

Some people say the way to conquer your fear of something is to get closer to it and not let it take over your thoughts. However, I cannot imagine being close enough to a palmetto bug to make that fear go away. Sure, I've had to kill one by myself when I've been alone in the house; I mean, you do what you gotta do sometimes. But that doesn't mean that I have control over how I feel about them.

In fact, just a while back, I had one of the worst experiences with one. I had gone to the bathroom, and let me start out by saying that we'd had a lot of rainfall. It almost rained every day this particular month and that always makes them come around.

So there I was, sitting down and minding my own business, when I saw it—a big palmetto bug on the cabinet directly in front of me. Now in this situation, what can you do? If you move, it may move. You can't kill it because, believe me, those things are almost indestructible. You need a big shoe and a heavy hand, neither of which I had in the bathroom. If you spray it with something, not that I had anything handy, it'll run away first and you will either lose it or it may run at you and let's not forget, I was sitting on the toilet. I must have sat there for a minute or two frozen in fear. I didn't know whether to run, get up slowly, or call for help. I finally got up the courage to get up very slowly and, when I got enough distance between us, I yelled out, *"Help!"* at the top of my lungs. My husband came to rescue me, then he uttered those horrifying words you never want to hear. "I don't see it."

It wasn't gone at all. He simply misunderstood where I told him it was.

I don't know if I'll ever get over my fear of these bugs. I find them disgusting, vile, and the most awful things I can think of. There is honestly not much in the world that frightens me more than a palmetto bug and unfortunately, I live in an area that is full of them.

I can only arm myself with a multitude of chemicals, a broom (because I do not want to get up close to one in case I have to kill it so I beat it to death from a distance) and a husband who will kill them for me.

GEOFFERY AND THE GREAT GLASS ELEVATOR

Geoffery Crescent

So there it was; my nemesis. Hanging from the ceiling by a golden thread, a shimmering prism, clear right through. Yes, it was a glass elevator. And yes, that's the thing which scares me most in the whole world.

It's not what you'd call a popular phobia; I get that. It's not like a fear of heights or a fear of spiders; most of us have those ingrained into our psyche because of something called "preparedness."

In other words, our ancestors had to have some way of knowing those things were dangerous, and it's kind of come down through the years to us today. Not really the way to explain my fear of glass elevators; I'm pretty sure *Homo erectus* didn't have any problems with those. Now let's get one thing straight: I'm not really a fan of heights, either. Spiders I quite like, but heights make me go funny at the knees. Even seeing tall buildings on TV makes me feel a bit weird. But when it comes down to it, I'll fly in a plane without too much trouble and I quite enjoy a ride on a roller coaster. But glass elevators are just the ultimate no-no.

Most people find this incredibly odd. "It's not like a normal elevator, is it? You can see where you're going! Wouldn't want to get stuck in a normal elevator, it'd be all claustrophobic."

Thing is, I have been stuck in a glass elevator and I can tell you now it was hell!

There's a big shopping centre near where I live; Cascades is its name. There were two storeys of shops on top of the restaurant floor, arranged in hoops, very white, very bland. As a ten-year-old girl, I went for the chocolate doughnut shop. I can only presume my father went for the eight-storey car park. In the centre of all these gleaming white hoops was a long, elegantly crafted clear tube, reaching from ceiling to floor; the shaft for a gleaming glass elevator. I used to quite like going down in it; going up would trigger my fear of heights, but going down was fine, just enough to trigger a little thrill of vertigo within me, and I used to like watching each of the hooped storeys pass us by as we got closer to our destination. But then, one day, it just stopped, part way through its descent, in between floors eight and nine. Between two floors, with no way out.

It's making my palms sweaty twelve years later, just reminiscing about it. I can't remember how many people there were in the elevator with me and my dad. There must have been quite a few, though, because I remember them all, including my dad, laughing about it.

"Oh ho, ho, ho, we're trapped in the elevator, better press the emergency button, chaps!"

Whatever direction I looked in, I could see exactly how far away we were from the floor and it terrified me. I settled for resting my forehead against the cool panes of glass with my eyes squeezed tight shut. A voice came over a tannoy, telling us not to worry, they'd get it moving again in just a moment. I never found out what the exact problem was. My dad, who's not brilliant at reading feelings at the best of times, completely misjudged how I felt about the situation and decided to mutter vaguely at me that it was all a big adventure.

Robin Hood is a big adventure, *Star Wars,* the Hobbit. None of those features people getting stuck inside big, see-through elevators. Well, maybe *Star Wars* does, but that's beside my point. What I wanted right then was a hug, on flat, opaque ground.

I remember so clearly how I couldn't hear anything properly; my ears were filled with a mixture of buzzing and the pounding of my heart. When we finally begun to move again, it must have been fifteen minutes or so we were stuck, but to use an old adage, it had felt like a lifetime; the relief that washed over me was cold and palpable. Although, that was probably mostly my sweat…

And so, gracefully and inexorably, we headed down, down betwixt the hoops of Cascades, down until we reached the third floor. Now, this wasn't our stop, so my dad motioned for me to stay on, until we got to the bottom, as it were. Unfortunately for me, it seemed that fate was not on our side that day because someone on the top floor must have called the elevator first. For up we went. Back up to the ninth floor, then back down to the third and then…you've guessed it, back up to the ninth. You know how in cartoons, when characters' legs turn into wibbly lines if they get scared? That's how mine felt that day. At that moment, I informed my dad point blank that I wasn't going any farther, stomped doggedly out of the elevator and headed down the nine flights of stairs to the bottom. I didn't once look back to see if he was following.

So that's how it all started. From that day forth, I haven't been able to look at a glass elevator without feeling a bit funny. Okay, so maybe it's not something that affects my every waking moment like some people's fears do, but when it arises, it's crippling. The few times I was forced, as a child, into another glass elevator, I promptly became dizzy or had a horrible panic attack. A more curious facet of the phobia is that I cannot stand anything high up with a lattice pattern, similar to the one on the glass elevator at Cascades. I remember ascending to the top of the Basilica on a school trip to Rome and promptly fainting because the viewing platform was rimmed with a wire net. I even got a strange sensation climbing up the lattice structures in *Assassin's Creed*, which is about as far removed from reality as you can get.

A few months ago, my partner and I had tickets to a show at London's South Bank Centre. After half an hour's wandering round the building which is, by the way, gorgeous, imposing, and ridiculously hard to navigate, we decided to ask a guide which way our stage was.

"Oh, it's easy," he said, "just hop in that elevator and it's right at the top."

The behemoth to which he gestured to was, of course, made of glass. My boyfriend, who is well versed in all my bizarre nuances, knew at once that this would be no good and asked for the alternate route.

"But you can just get in there!" The guide was utterly confused as to why two patrons, already late for their show, would refuse to get in an elevator right beside them that would take them straight to their destination, but there it was. *There has to be an alternate route*, I was thinking desperately, sweat beginning to break out under my velvet jacket. *They must have something else, in case the elevator breaks down.*

"I suppose if you really want, you can walk the long way round," the guide finally offered, eyeing up my purple stilettos. He did, of course, offer us an alternate route, and I was grateful to finally have the damned thing out of my sight.

I would love not to have this fear, I would love it. It might not seem like a big thing to you, or even a real thing, but I think that everyone has at least one thing that is absolutely petrifying, and this is mine.

One day, I know that I'll get in one without feeling like I'm on the brink of collapse, but that won't be because someone has forced me in, or told me there's no other option. It'll be in my terms. And I feel like I've already started making steps.

I'd had a truly crappy day, one of those where just everything seems to go wrong. And I'd found myself in a bookshop with two of my friends, a bookshop with a tiny glass elevator between its two floors. The stairs round it were twisted in such a way that you could hardly see through the glass, but seeing it still made me feel scared. But just then, it was the right moment. I knew I had to do something to make my awful day seem worthwhile and so, with a hand on each of my friend's arms, I went down a single floor in a glass elevator.

When I stepped out, I was shaking, but utterly elated. I knew at that point that this wasn't something that was going to define me for the rest of my life.

I live in a city called Portsmouth, which is home to an impressive piece of architecture known as the Spinnaker Tower. It's famous for its glass floors and outdoor elevator, which is often known to stop halfway up the tower. Thinking about it now makes me feel horrible, tiny creatures clawing at my stomach, bile rising in my throat, every muscle in my body tensing up. Perhaps I'll never understand why anyone would choose to make an elevator out of glass, a material that seems to me to be so fragile, so easily shattered. But I'd like to believe one day I'll be able to think about it without getting scared.

ICHOR

Alyn Day

I wasn't always afraid of spiders. In fact, as a very young child I had two pet tarantulas named Crystal and Christina, captured natives of the desert I called my home. There are pictures of me in a pretty red dress, around age four or five, playing with them, letting them climb and crawl over my lap or across the little table where I drew and colored. I had no reason to fear them; they were calm if I was calm. They were furry, like a teddy bear, and rounded, with long legs and comically large abdomens. Even their fangs looked relatively harmless to my small eyes, held as they were behind a set of fuzzy, soft-looking mandibles.

I'd had no bad experiences with spiders, nothing to discourage my enjoyment of them. In fact, I had spent countless hours watching a large, rosy orb weaver building and rebuilding a web outside my window. Spiders were endlessly fascinating. I had books about them, as I did each of my wild-caught pets, and I found their hunting and eating habits interesting and unusual. I watched documentaries and read issues of *National Geographic* about everything from trapdoor spiders to the venomous funnel-webs of Australia and the bird-eating tarantula spiders of South America. I would rush to defend any spider that someone was going to smash with a shoe, catching them and delivering them to the freedom and relative safety of the outdoors.

There are people who will tell you that fear is learned, not necessarily instinctive. I'm of the opinion that some fears are like scars born of distress, lingering marks of something traumatic that happened to us at one point or another, which forever mar our lives and our views of the world by association.

As the daughter of two military parents, I did a good deal of moving and traveling when I was a child. Changes of scenery and entirely new environments weren't uncommon for me, and I tended to adapt well to whatever surroundings I was presented with. I was a curious child, not at all squeamish or fearful like some little girls. There were few things I loved more than being let loose outdoors with a few jars and a butterfly net to ensnare some new flora and fauna to decorate my room with for a few days, before releasing it back into the wild and beginning the cycle anew.

My siblings didn't share my enthusiasm for insects and arachnids, a trait that had earned me the nickname "Bug." They would, however, pause to inspect whatever I had managed to catch, once it was secured in some sort of container, meaning that they were relatively safe from whatever harm a large green caterpillar or a little black snake could do.

Entomology wasn't my only interest. I was, after all, a child, albeit one with unusual hobbies. I shared my siblings' desire to run and play and roughhouse like any other tot.

The incident which would cause me to turn away from creatures I had once loved and admired occurred on a balmy spring day in rural Indiana in my seventh year. It was a beautiful morning, the sky was clear and blue, dotted with wispy white clouds that promised little respite from the bright, warm sun, let alone any sort of precipitation. The grass was cool and green, still wet with morning dew, a phenomenon I was enchanted by, having just moved from the very different environment of New Mexico's dry, sandy landscape. I enjoyed taking off my shoes and socks and letting the wet grass tickle my feet.

My younger brother, two years my junior but much smaller in stature than I was, due to his premature birth, had been begging me to play tag with him through the sunflower field near the edge of our property. I was enjoying the wet grass, the fresh green scent of spring, and the singing of the birds in nearby trees, but when he raced up and tagged me on the arm with a joyous cry of "You're it!" I gave chase.

Though he was much shorter, more slight, and asthmatic, he was quick. I found myself struggling to try and catch up; thus, my attention was completely focused on the little towheaded boy in front of me, and completely diverted from my surroundings. In an unfamiliar environment, that can mean unexpected consequences.

Unbeknownst to me, and unnoticed due to my single-minded focus on catching my kid brother, a large spider had built a web between two sunflowers. It was an orb weaver, much like the one I had watched build elaborate webs outside my bedroom window in New Mexico, but this one was of a different variety. It was larger, for one thing, and narrower, with a black and yellow segmented body and long legs attached to an almond-shaped thorax above a much narrower abdomen. The spider's web was too high to catch my brother; he ran right under it and probably wouldn't have known it existed at all, if not for what happened next.

As you might have guessed, it was at just the right height to catch me as I ran after my younger sibling, almost exactly level with my face. The spider was large, even for orb weavers in that particular area of the country; its legs stretched almost entirely across my face. It had built a lovely and quite sizable web, hoping to snare a juicy dragonfly or perhaps a swallowtail, but instead, it caught me.

Being a small child, I panicked. I began frantically trying to get it off my face, clawing at my cheeks and forehead. Unfortunately, the web did an excellent job of pinning the spider to my small face like some kind of living Halloween mask. It was probably just as horrified as I was, if not more so, so of course, it bit me.

I don't really know what happened after that. My brother was nearly as terrified as I was, and being four years old, he responded by crying. I think I must have passed out, from terror, from shock, from something else entirely, I can't be sure. What I do know is that I awoke in the back of an ambulance with an oxygen mask strapped to my face and no trace of the spider. Around me were two paramedics, my brother, my mother, and one of our new neighbors, whom, I later learned, had called the ambulance for me.

I was taken to the local hospital and thoroughly examined. The emergency room doctor gave my mother some topical cream for the bite and jokingly called me Rudolph, as the red swelling on my nose had enlarged enough for me to see it, if I crossed my eyes slightly. My brother responded by clinging to me almost protectively, as if he could somehow prevent the events of that day from happening by embracing me. I didn't say much. I was thinking, stuck inside my own head, as I so often was as a kid and even still today. Part of me was still in shock, I suppose.

I wondered why all of the good karma I had amassed among the spider kingdom, thanks to having rescued so many of its members, hadn't saved me. I couldn't rid myself of the feeling of that poor thing twitching on my face, the sticky prison of its web pinning it to me like some people pinned butterflies to display boards. I wondered what had happened to it, but found that I really didn't want to know. It hurt me to imagine that someone had killed it, that it was dead because of me and my clumsiness and lack of attention to my surroundings, but at the same time, I was also feeling something relatively new—fear. I was afraid that it had crawled off amid the chaos and was waiting somewhere, lurking in the shadows, preparing to exact its revenge on me for something that hadn't been deliberate on my part.

For several years after that day, the sight of a spider, even a tiny little harmless house spider, would bring on severe panic attacks, causing my heart rate to speed out of control, cold sweat to break out on my skin, and uncontrollable trembling, dizziness and nausea.

It was difficult to explain to friends and coworkers why I couldn't just crush the offending beast with a tissue and move on. More than once, my fear was treated as a joke. People would put fake spiders on my desk or in my books, thinking it was funny, when really it was anything but.

Academically, I knew that there was little a plain old everyday house spider could do to harm me, but for some reason, my brain refused to accept that, spiraling out of control sometimes at the mere mention of a stray arachnid.

It wasn't until several years later, when I was twenty-four, that I would eventually overcome that fear and resume my previous spider-rescuing ways.

I came down with a severe liver infection and was hospitalized for several days. For much of my initial time in the emergency room, I was unconscious and being fed intravenously.

When I finally awoke, I was very weak and disoriented. It was nighttime; I could see moonlight filtering in through the shades on my window, hear strange beeping from around me, but I didn't have the strength to move much more than my eyelids. I didn't know where I was, what had happened, or even what day it was. As I struggled to lift my head, I caught sight of something dark on the white sheets over my weakened body. It was about the size of my thumbnail, and it was moving.

As my eyes began to find focus, I realized that the mysterious blotch was, in fact, a spider.

Perhaps it was my weakened state of being, or perhaps it was the morphine that was being administered via IV, but I didn't feel the normal panic attack coming on. Instead, I felt sort of serene, peaceful. Without the trappings of terror I'd been bound by for so long, I found that the senses of wonder and curiosity about my eight-legged visitor were still present. I proceeded to watch the little spider, all the while drifting in and out of sleep, until I opened my eyes and found the room lit by sunshine and fluorescent lights, a nurse standing over me as she changed the IV bag. I looked for my arachnid companion, but didn't see her.

Wherever she went, I remain grateful to her for reminding me once again of life's wonders, even the ones with eight legs.

ONE THOUSAND EIGHTY DEGREES

J.T. Evans

In the span of one thousand eighty degrees of rotation and less than fifteen seconds, my life changed forever. At the time, I was an invulnerable, worries-to-the-wind fifteen-year-old. Nothing could touch me. Nothing could destroy me. Like all teenagers, I knew everything and would live forever. The accident in the perfect early-morning hours of August 8, 1988 warped my psyche and destroyed my invulnerability in a way I'll never forget.

My older stepsister, Big M, "borrowed" her father's GMC Jimmy for a joyride into town to visit her boyfriend-of-the-week. With school being out, I was free to roam the countryside in which I lived until all hours of the early morning. The number one rule in my freedom was, "Don't come crying to Mommy if you get hurt."

I lived by that rule and enjoyed the liberty of walking under the cool West Texas skies, staring up at the constellations slowly sliding across in the inky darkness.

My friend, C, and my younger stepsister, Little M, walked the nights with me as we found little ways to get in trouble without causing problems for our neighbors. As we walked along the country road we lived on, the roar of an engine behind us caught our attention. Out of reflex, we dove for the scrub brush in the bar ditch beside the road. Our reactions were too slow this time, and the vehicle screeched to a stop. We weren't worried about kidnappings or such, but if a police officer caught us out at night, he would be sure to haul us home, wake our parents, and ask lots of stupid questions. It was a hassle I didn't want to repeat.

Big M's familiar voice called out from the stopped car. "Will you guys get out of the dirt and hop in? Want to go for a ride?"

With relief, we stood up and dusted ourselves off. The three of us clambered into the Jimmy, and Big M lit the tires up as we roared down the dirt roads of the rural community. Music blared from the stereo as tires slipped back and forth on the caliche roadways. From the sound of Big M's blabbering, I could tell she wasn't sober. I'm not sure what she had done at her boyfriend-of-the-week's house, but the scent of cigarette smoke, sex, and booze mingled in the tight cab of the SUV. The only thing I could think was that Big M was so going to be busted for stinking up her dad's Jimmy.

We roamed the back roads and country lanes long enough for the excitement of "borrowing" my stepfather's car to turn to boredom and apathy. The midnight hour rolled by, and Big M continued her random wanderings through the country. Different roads of asphalt and dirt became lost in the red taillights and in the darkness of the night. I became thoroughly turned around and lost, but C seemed to know where we were at.

Big M careened around a dirt corner and slid to a stop with the dust swirling in the headlights. Little M cried in fright from the front seat as I was tossed across the back seat into C. Tired of being thrown to and fro, I quickly threw on my seatbelt. C followed suit. Little did we know this minor measure of safety would save our lives.

I called to the front seat over the din of the music. "Slow down a bit! This Jimmy is top-heavy. You're going to flip us!"

Big M ignored my pleas and tore off down the dirt road at an amazing clip. Halfway down the country mile, she began to swerve back and forth on the road. Cries of glee escaped the lips of Big and Little M alike. C glanced at me with a nervous smile, and I'm certain the color had drained from my face.

The next fifteen seconds of my life are permanently ingrained in memory. Every little detail. Every little motion. Every little sensation. It's all burned into me and will be there, physically and emotionally, until the day I pass from this world.

Big M lost control of the Jimmy. The bar ditch on the left side of the road loomed deep and wide in the headlights. In the blink of an eye, a shuddering *thump* passed through the vehicle and our bodies as the SUV slammed into the far side of the ditch. We had built up so much speed and momentum that the far wall of the ditch did little to impede our forward progress. The upslope of the ditch's far side acted as a ramp and launched us into the air.

The world spun around us. We landed upside-down on the front-right corner of the Jimmy. The roof caved in just far enough to ding Little M on the top of her head, but she wouldn't even need stitches for the cut. After the screeching crunch of metal ceased, we continued to flip and roll. We rolled a total of three times, for a total pirouette of one thousand eighty degrees.

Just as the gut-wrenching crash started, my motorcycle racing training kicked in. I had been taught that during a wreck, the best thing to do is relax. The energy exerted on the human body during a crash of any magnitude is so great that fighting physics will result in more grievous injuries. Just as the first roll started, I took a deep breath, held it, and willed my limbs to flop about my body under the control of the centrifugal forces of the roll.

My feet careened about the floorboards, attached to gummy-like legs, and my arms slung over and around my head like earthworms dying on a sunbaked sidewalk during triple-digit temperatures.

As the Jimmy thump-thumped its way across the cotton field we ended up in, I distinctly remember Little M calling out Big M's name. The terrified, little-girl scream still echoes in my nightmares to this day. Somewhere in the midst of the drawn out howl, I encountered a sensation that is most difficult to describe, but I will do my best to paint the picture of permanent nerve damage.

My right arm went cold and numb.

Forever.

A wave of frigid terror extended from just below my shoulder to my fingertips, in my nerves' one final gasp at life before being severed forever from the lump of gray mass that resides between my ears.

Glass exploded inward from a shattered pane as the SUV rolled one last time.

A gently rocking motion, like a mother cradling a newborn babe, ended Little M's caterwaul of panic. The Jimmy had somehow ended up on its wheels and the momentum from the horrific crash caused it to rock back and forth on its springs. Somewhere in the crash, the dome light came on and shed its yellow glare down in the vehicle.

I immediately saw all of the blood.

I thought it was someone else's. There was no way *I* could be the one hurt. I was invulnerable, after all. Right?

Wrong.

I asked everyone to sound off and tell me where they were hurt. Big M, Little M, and C all sounded off that they were okay. I didn't believe them for an instant. With a shaky voice, I called out, "There's blood in the car and it came from someone."

I tried to motion with both of my arms, but only the left one responded. I don't know what I was about to say next because the words caught in my throat. I realized I was the one hurt.

I was the one pouring my lifeblood out into the battered GMC Jimmy.

Damn.

Since we had "borrowed" my stepfather's car, we knew we were in deep trouble. Big M worried the keys like a rabid dog in an effort to dislodge them from the ignition switch. All the while, she cried, "I'm so going to get grounded."

I growled at her. "Leave the damn keys. I'm bleeding and I don't know how badly I'm hurt. We have to get back to the house and see what I can do to sew this up."

Even though bloodied and broken, I still thought myself immortal. I figured a few cheap stitches using my mom's sewing kit would close me up and we could maybe hide the fact that all of us were in the Jimmy.

After the four of us clambered from the ruins of the SUV, I reached back to see how badly my arm was wounded. When the second knuckle of my fingers entered the gaping wound in my arm, I knew it was bad. Real bad. Something in my brain snapped at that moment. I stood at death's door and he welcomed me in. Not ready to cross that threshold just yet, I somehow managed to tear off my t-shirt and use it as a makeshift tourniquet where my arm merged with my shoulder. The resulting knot of cloth from tying off the t-shirt as tightly as I could went *inside my arm,* as a crude compress to try to staunch the flow of blood. I can thank the Boy Scouts for these skills and training. Without them, I may very well have crossed the doorway into death's realm, never to return again.

The march back to our rural home began. I didn't think. I just acted. One foot in front of the other. About half a mile down the road, we reached one of the main roads that was paved. It would lead us straight to our house, a little over a mile away.

That's when we spotted the police officer turning the corner. Someone living in the remote area must have heard the crash and called 911. Out of reflex, we all dove for cover. How the cop didn't see us, I'm not sure. It must have been the utter darkness of the new moon and lack of city lights that saved us from being spotted. As he rolled past our hiding spot, he saw the Jimmy and drove toward it. When he exited his cruiser to march the forty yards to the wreckage, we made a run for it.

After crossing the paved country road, we made our way deep into the soft dirt of the plowed cotton fields. Running in the darkness, Big M and Little M stayed together. Somehow, C stayed at my side. Once we were sufficiently deep into the field not to be seen from the road, we called for one another. The Ms made their way back to us, and I had my first experience with body control.

I knew that if I kept my heart rate up at a high pace, it would do nothing more than pump my life out of my gaping wound and kill me. I willed my heart to slow. I commanded my breathing to return to a normal depth. Through sheer force of mind over body, I calmed myself. I had no other choice.

Once we regrouped, we started trudging eastward through the thick soil of the farmers' lands. Things went well for about half a mile, and then we ran into the security fence dividing one piece of property from another. The six-foot tall chain link fence was topped by another foot of barbed wire. I never did understand why someone would build such a contraption in the middle of a cotton field, but the reasonings didn't matter to me at that moment. All I knew is that I had to climb the seven-foot tall barrier with a single arm.

I urged C to climb over first, to catch the Ms as they came over the top. Next went Big M and then Little M. Why I didn't go over in the middle of the pack where I could have some help on both sides is beyond me. I guess chivalry isn't dead. Not yet, at least. I managed to climb the fence with my two good feet, and my one good arm. Rough is hardly a harsh enough word to describe the difficulty of the situation, but it comes close.

Once on the other side, we made good time back to our house. When we reached the place, I told C to head home, get in his bed, and play dumb. I didn't want him getting in trouble like the rest of us were surely going to. We made our way inside, and I went straight to the bathroom. Turning the back of my damaged arm to the mirror so I could see my wound, I gently unpacked the cloth knot from the innards of my arm and released the tourniquet.

The sight of the bloody gash, white bone, and torn flesh of my arm almost made me pass out on the spot. Again, I willed myself to stay standing, so that I wouldn't die on the spot. Death couldn't have me. Yet.

I surged from the bathroom, then snatched the phone from Little M's hands. I didn't know who was on the other line, but I practically screamed into the phone, "She's okay! I'm the only one hurt."

Then I hung up the phone and called 911. Somehow, I was extremely calm throughout the process of requesting help from an ambulance. It felt as if I were ordering pizza, not saving my life. It was just something that had to be done to guarantee my continued survival, so I did it without fuss or muss.

Somewhere during all of this, my stepfather and mother woke up to the chaos created by two scared teenagers and a crying adolescent.

By this time, about thirty minutes had passed. I waited for another fifteen for the ambulance to show up. During this entire time, Little M did nothing more than cry and babble incoherently. Big M and her father screamed at each other about the events of the night. My mother and I sat in the bathroom while she cried, "There's a hunk of your arm missing!"

She wasn't quite right. The gap in my arm wasn't missing tissue, but just a huge slice in my arm. The human body is wound so tightly that if you cut it deep enough, the wound will naturally pull open. It makes for a ghastly sight, that's for sure.

The ambulance driver and his paramedic team showed up and I almost got into a fistfight with the paramedic. He took one look at my arm, damn near lost his supper all over me, and then started repeating his mantra, "You should be dead by now!"

I had to keep saying, "But I'm not. Let's go to the hospital."

Eventually, we went to the hospital just like I wanted to.

By the time the emergency medical teams at the hospital were finished with me, I had more than twenty stitches in my right ear, a little fewer than twenty stitches in my head behind my ear, and around twenty-five stitches in my right hand. The explosion of glass from the untempered right rear window had shredded my extremities.

A day or so later (morphine will mess with your space-time continuum in a serious way), I was wheeled into the operating suite with three doctors at my side. One orthopedic surgeon was going to put me back together, with the help of a vascular surgeon and a neurosurgeon. Five hours after they started, I was back in one piece.

It turned out the cut on the back of my arm sliced entirely through my triceps, humerus (upper arm bone), and nicked the inside layers of my biceps. Somehow, the vital parts of my upper arm were left mostly intact. The brachial artery and ulnar vein had been left intact by the slicing action of the shards of glass that maimed me. The brachial plexus, which is a large bundle of nerves traveling alongside the ulnar vein, had been slightly damaged, but had been repaired to the best of the neurosurgeon's abilities.

To this day, I suffer from near-constant nerve pain in my arm, and there are times when scar tissue will shift to the point that my arm "falls dead." During these hours-long episodes, I cannot move the arm, feel the arm, or get good circulation to and from the limb. When this happens in my sleep, I suffer from terrible nightmares triggered by the physical sensations of my arm "falling dead" on me as I slumber.

Earlier, I mentioned mental scars. It may sound like the physical price I paid for that joyride was enough to punish me for my youthful stupidity.

It was not.

For some people, the sight of something is enough to evoke terror. For others, it may be a smell, thought, or touch. For me, it's a sensory situation. When I'm in a car that suddenly swerves left to right or right to left, I panic. When I'm in a car that suddenly drifts a slight bit, such as on ice or dirt roads, I panic. When a car that I'm in takes a turn too fast and lurches to one side, or even gets on two wheels, I panic.

This panic for me is a full emotional breakdown as I flash back to the early morning hours of the eighth day of the eighth month of the eighty-eighth year of the twentieth century of the year of our Lord. I fully experience every second of sound, sight, motion, pain, feeling, lack of feeling, and emotion that I felt during those fifteen seconds of chaos and terror. I break down into a babbling, incoherent fifteen-year-old screaming about horrors in the night and blood in my arm. There's no pulling me out of the visions of terror until they run their course. I have no idea how long this takes, but I've had friends tell me that I was "out of it" for "a few minutes" each time this has happened.

I have one upside to these flashbacks. If I *know* beforehand that the vehicle is about to drift, slide, swerve, or tilt, then I can prepare my mind and force it not to freak out. Only with this split-second of mental preparation can I keep from flashing back to that horrible night of blood, pain, and darkness.

I come from a line of racecar drivers on my mother's side, and somehow have inherited the gene that allows me to be able to *feel my car* through my feet and hands on the controls and my butt in the seat. Through these feelings, I know what my car is about to do next, even if I'm not in full control. It's through these sensations and my predictions that allow me to control any panic-inducing thoughts before they strike. This is a blessing, because I can't imagine what might happen to me, and those around me, if I were to lose control of my mind while attempting to drive a car. I'm certain a new wreck, with new nightmares to follow, would ensue.

I'm not sure what kind of phobia a psychologist would call this, or if they would classify this as PTSD or something similar. All I know is that if there is even a hint that a car I'm in might flip or lose control, I suffer a traumatic flashback that causes me to relive one of the worst nights of my life.

One physical thing that I carry with me every time I move is the t-shirt I wore that night. It's the t-shirt that saved my life. I'm never getting rid of it, even though it doesn't fit anymore. I pull it out on August 8 each year and look at the holes in the fabric, trace my fingers along the lines of the bloodstains, and close my eyes to remember. I have to do this, so that I don't forget one very important fact of my life.

I'm not invulnerable.

MANY PHOBIA

Jay Sutter

I first met Jane during the major power outage of October 29, 2012. The unexpected snowstorm here in New England devastated most people's lives. Many went without power for two entire weeks. People without any major phobias or fears fared fine. I imagine people with fears of the dark, fear of the future, fear of freezing, and maybe even fear of social situations had a much tougher time.

I was asked by Jane's daughter, Iris, to help clear their yard of the heavy debris that fell that fateful day. Iris confided that this was a very big step for Jane, to ask a perfect stranger to help. It was an act of faith for Jane to ask for any help from anyone, or allow someone to help.

Jane is a very hard worker in a local industrial complex. She goes to work, comes home, does yard work, and truly enjoys comfortably relaxing with a book. This is her norm, her safety, her contentment. Anything that changes this pattern might invoke uncomfortableness, anxiety, or in certain situations, a panic attack. I do not know Jane well enough to comprehend all her fears or phobias, but she has told me some of them, and I have witnessed others.

I write this piece to try to shed light on people who may be more sensitive than I am, to attempt to better understand, to empathize, and to appreciate their uniqueness. Hopefully, we can acknowledge and help in the healing process. I sense many phobias have a root in our childhoods. Something just did not sit well with us, or maybe a traumatic event or set of events occurred that has semi-permanently become part of our personality. I hope that I can explain Jane's precious, sweet, and seemingly fragile ways.

I called Jane's cellphone number that her daughter gave me while traveling to her small town in Connecticut. A gentle but confident voice answered. I asked how far south on Route 178 the house was located. Jane gave me a detailed description of landmarks. She asked me key questions to find out where I was on the road. I got confused by the numbers on the mailboxes because I was still in Massachusetts, but thought I was in Connecticut already. The number schemes were quite similar—1681, 1679, 1675—and I was looking for 1677. But there was no 1677. I turned back and headed north. Jane calmly told me that I was not in Connecticut yet. She amazingly kept her cool, while I was frustrated from too much coffee, too little sleep, too much shoveling the night before, and too little sense of direction. Jane kept me on the phone until I saw her standing in front of her mailbox, flagging me down. Whew.

So, you are probably wondering why I haven't mentioned Jane's phobias yet.

Jane has adapted quite well concerning her fears. This is a testament to her continued vigilance in dealing with them, and to her intelligence. I can't say what she was thinking while we were on the phone, but I imagine she was quite scared for me. I have seen how very concerned and worried she is about her two grown children. She needs to know where they are at all times and wants them to stay close, geographically. Jane wants them to tell her how long they will be out. She is not controlling in this behavior. I know that she is so very loving, so very sensitive, so deeply tied to her children that she requires it for her peace of mind. Her children are her extension, and I wish that all mothers and most fathers would be this way. Our world would be a more magnificent and gentle place to live. However, some things in this world are harsh, and rough, and unexpected.

Jane was taken out of her element due to the storm. She had no power. She used candles for light. She cooked food on the outdoor barbecue grill. She lit fires every day in the fire pit. She took showers at the local school gymnasium. Jane has a phobia about fires in her home, mostly electrical-type. She usually unplugs all the appliances and all the lamps before leaving the house. She always double-checks the stove knobs to make sure they are all off. It is her level of anxiety that is unusual. She will worry that she didn't check all the appliances, or that she should not have left the living room lamps on while she went out for the night.

Jane gets very upset if her daughter goes to do some apparently "dangerous" activity such as snowboarding or rock climbing. Iris has a good amount of experience with both and does these activities with experts who are very safety conscious. Jane doesn't want to know where her daughter is going, yet on the other hand, needs to know so she can still feel connected. It is quite a quandary. I suggested to Iris that she write down where she is going in a notebook for her Mom to check if she feels the need. That way, Jane is able to gain control of her fears.

I rolled my old red Chevy truck on to the yard. The grass was wet, so my two-wheel drive truck almost got stuck. I revved the engine a tad, just enough to tear up a spot in the middle of the lawn. *Oooops*. Jane didn't seem to flinch about this, which I thought amazing. Many women I have been around would have yelled at me. Jane was calm and sweet. She said she needed to plant new grass again anyway, and she was going to expand her vegetable garden in that spot.

I loaded a bunch of evergreen branches in the back of my truck. Jane was very concerned that I didn't overload it. I believe now that she was dealing with a phobia, a fear that something bad could happen if there were too many branches stacked up. Again, it would be out of caring. Iris's boyfriend John showed up. He and I worked in tandem, loading my truck up. On one occasion, I repositioned a large branch and it smashed my window. Jane shrieked.

She immediately offered to pay for a new window. I told her not to bother, that I needed a newer one anyway. Jane was very insistent, and seemed very upset for a long time after. In fact, two weeks after the incident, she was asking about the window. Was this part of a phobia? Did she want everything to be okay, to be normalized? I drove around for a month without that small window. Jane was relieved when she found out that I had indeed replaced it.

Jane confided that her home and yard are her oasis. Many people are homebodies, but I believe that the reason Jane stays home is that she does not like going out in society. She is so sensitive that the strong negative emotions in the gas station or at the library would create fear and anxiety for her internally. She admitted that she would not eat any food at a restaurant. She did work in food services before, but for her not to eat at all, anywhere other than home, is quite unusual. Jane once went to a Bertucci's Restaurant to eat out, a few years ago. The counters were filthy. Someone found a hair in the food. One of the glasses had shards in the drink. There was something else that was disgusting, Jane told me, but I forget what it was. That one bad experience framed her phobia. She will probably never eat out again.

Jane has a deep fear of a certain hill in Connecticut. It is a substantial hill, and she confided that when she has to stop at the red light on that hill, she hyperventilates, begins shaking, and experiences deep fear. She is afraid the car will roll backward and she will lose control of the vehicle.

Of course, I told her about my harrowing experience in Japan on a hill. It was winter. My four-cylinder Datsun Sunny contained my wife, my one-year-old daughter, and me. We were halfway up the mile-long hill, and the road was icy. Our little car stopped at a certain point, and began sliding backward without my permission. I had the gas pedal to the floor and we were still traveling in reverse, due to the ice.

Quickly, I spun my wheel to the left, reversing into a side street on our left. I waited for the traffic to subside. I then revved the car in a diagonal switchback pattern, crossing into the other lane to get to the top of the hill. By explaining this crisis to her, I thought that it might show empathy for her phobia of hills. I honestly believe it did help her. She exclaimed to her daughter, "See, it can be dangerous on a hill!"

Jane and I had further discussions about this fear or phobia. I told her that I already wrote a piece on my phobia called *Dog-O-Teeth-O-Phobia*. I believe this fact helped her, too, to know others have phobias. It is all right to share them, to be yourself. In fact, Jane came up with the idea that phobias can be learned. She said her phobia about appliances being unplugged and thoughts of possible fires came from her late husband. Interesting. Maybe that means if a phobia can be passed on, then it can be unlearned, as well.

So I was invited to join Jane, Iris, Iris' boyfriend John, and John's parents, Allan and Irene, to watch a comedian at a club. Iris won free tickets from work and everyone had to be present at the club to redeem the tickets. A couple hours before we were to meet, Iris called me. She said that we may not be able to see the show, that it was not guaranteed. I told her we could make alternate plans if it didn't work out. Iris wasn't sure if Jane would go or not, due to her fears of going out. I arrived at Jane and Iris' home. Jane wasn't sure if she wanted to go. I encouraged her by saying, "Life is too short, give it a try." She relented and decided to go with us.

Of course, Jane checked the knobs on the stove before we left. After thirty seconds down the road, Jane wondered if she should've unplugged the living room lights. Iris asked if she wanted to turn back. Jane said no. Wow, what a big leap of faith.

We arrived at the club, inside a local mall. The man at the booth told Iris she was supposed to call four or five days in advance to reserve the free seats. What? Jane's face turned red and she was visibly upset. She talked to the booth operator and he turned her away. Jane voiced that she should be home reading a book. The other three people arrived and I suggested we go eat, instead.

They chose Bertucci's, the same place where Iris and Jane had a horrible experience. Jane gave in and at least sat quietly at the table during dinner with a glass of water. Jane and I had previously decided on certain code words to indicate if the other was misbehaving or being too blunt. My word for her was Blue Hills or Blue Sox. She would say Red Sox if I was out of line. For some reason, I kept jabbering and joking. Jane didn't use the code word, she just mouthed *shut up*. Wow. I guess I was unnerving her. So I made a concerted effort not to say much after that. The only major fear I detected for Jane was when a fruit fly buzzed near her face. She shrieked. I tried to swat it more than once. I really wanted to help her overcome her fears.

After dinner, we decided to go to a place called Nomads. It is an unusual mix of an arcade that had the following features: video games, miniature golf, a mechanical bull, bar, a climbing wall, a boxing ring, basketball courts, a whirling dervish, bumper cars, and other various games. We did not know how to get to the place, but someone had a rough idea. I decided to call 411 to ask for an address.

The girl on the other end told me, "It's on Wooo..wilth road."

I asked, "Did you say, Warwilth?"

The operator repeated, "Woo..worth."

I asked, "Woolworth?" The operator hung up.

I called Nomads.

The girl at Nomads gave me complicated directions as Iris paused in the left turn lane. Jane yelled, "You have to turn left," as another vehicle whizzed by us on the right. Jane asked me what the Nomad girl said. I could not remember any of her directions except that we had to turn left. So I called 411 again. A man answered. He told me that Nomads was on Bidwell Road. I asked him to spell it, just to make sure.

Iris pulled out her GPS and punched in the address. The GPS took us on a circuitous route through the black forest. Jane was afraid of the deep, dark woods all around us. The party behind followed us in their car. Iris did not want me to tell John that she used the GPS. I guess he frowned upon it. Later on, Irene continuously grilled me on why the 411 operator gave me directions on the phone. I didn't have the heart to say we used GPS. I let her wonder. Sorry. Red Sox.

We entered the front doors of Nomads. Lights and sounds bombarded us, similar to a casino feeling—overstimulating. Jane and I felt the same woozy effects. John lined up to ride the mechanical bull while Jane suddenly said that she needed a drink. So I escorted her to the adjoining bar. John's parents came with us.

Jane then confided to me, "Do you see those strange people in the bull riding room? Who are they and why are they just sitting there? I couldn't take them being there; that is why I need a drink. Who are they? The Bull Watchers?"

I laughed and looked across the bull riding room. There were about eight rather large women drinking beer and sitting dull-faced. They looked like hillbillies. I guess they were posse from a private party next door to the bull riding room. I had to agree that it was a very strange sight. I decided against riding the bull at that moment. I didn't want the Bull Watchers to look at me. They were not normal. Was Jane's phobia influencing me?

Jane asked me if I wanted a Jägermeister. I said fine, I would see it as medicine. Jane seemed to calm down a little while we were in the bar area. I only had to invoke the Blue Sox code word a couple times during this outing.

But at one point, Jane asked me about Irene. Jane said, "What is up with Irene's eyes? Did you notice that one of them seems like it's made of glass? Does she have a glass eye?"

I said, "I don't know. I didn't look right into her eyes."

I decided to go talk to Irene. I was going to investigate her eyes. I approached Irene and Allan as they watched a football game on TV. I asked them about the game and stared into Irene's eyes. By golly, her eyes seemed very glassy. The left eye seemed extra glossy. Was it made of glass? I went back to Jane.

Jane immediately asked me, "Well?"

I asked, "Well, what?"

"Does she have a glass eye or not?"

I said, "I don't know. One of her eyes seemed more glassy than the other."

What was happening here?

Irene suggested we play miniature golf. We all strolled to the blacklight golf room. Everybody's teeth were glowing. Allan and Irene golfed as a couple, ahead of everyone. The rest of us formed our own group. Jane and Iris were really great golfers. Halfway through the course, three big people interrupted our game by walking through us. They didn't even speak. They were teenagers.

Jane said, "Those were the children of the Bull Watchers."

I laughed.

Eventually, we made it outside the building to freedom and fresh cold air. Irene was smoking quietly. We parted ways.

Iris drove, with me in the front passenger seat, Jane in the back. As Iris backed out of her parking space, she turned the wheel to the left. The Subaru angled onto the round curbing and the front tire knocked over a landscaping stick. Simultaneously, the vehicle dropped a little as we landed back onto the pavement.

Jane screamed. "Didn't you see that stick? And we dropped about three feet."

I maintained, "The curbing was a poor design, and the stick should not have been there."

Iris agreed. Jane said something about breaking the law. I tried to smooth out the situation, to downplay it. We were all safe; the drop was less than a foot.

As we began to take a left from the parking lot on to the highway, Iris turned sharply, angling on to the wrong lane of the divided highway. I calmly pointed to the far side of the road, indicating she had to re-adjust. Jane began hyperventilating. I believe it was the whirling dervish that Iris rode on that affected her driving. She said that the spinning lights on the ride made her feel sick.

On the way back to their house, we discussed a lot of positive things. I thanked Jane for being so brave, for overcoming many of her fears. I told her she did good.

When we arrived at their house, Jane immediately got out of the car and ran to the front door. She said she had to use the bathroom, but I suspected she was craving her jammies and book. I didn't take it personally. Iris followed her mom and apologized via text message.

I think Jane will be all right, even with the shock therapy she had this night. I hope to spend more time with them, to help Jane to overcome her phobias. Of course, it is she who will have to decide if she wants to work on them. I am merely a helper. There is a prominent preacher that I have listened to on the radio, named Joyce Meyer. She has often said we ultimately are not supposed to have anxiety or to fear anything. She said it's okay to be afraid at times, but in order to accomplish anything, to be conquerors, then we should just "Do it afraid."

AUTOMATONOPHOBIA

Kay Brooks

Weirdly, I cannot say exactly what triggered my phobia, but I can remember the time when it intensified and I realised that what I had was worse than any normal fear. As a child, I had friends who were scared of spiders or getting lost. Both of these fears seemed reasonably rational to me; a spider could bite you, causing pain, and getting lost might mean not being able to find your family again. Despite being able to understand the fears that other children had, those fears didn't really affect me. The fact that I could happily handle spiders and would ride my bike as far as I could and then simply turn around and retrace my steps added to the general consensus that I was a "tomboy." That was fine by me! It was my excuse for climbing trees and getting dirty.

We were on a family holiday at the seaside resort of Blackpool, England, where incidentally I now live, when my phobia became obvious. Walking into The Pleasure Beach, an exciting theme park within the resort, the first thing I saw was the famous laughing clown. My little brother Tom went running over, putting his clammy hands on the glass and staring in at the perfectly still mannequin.

Clowns have never bothered me. I had one at my fifth birthday party and, although he turned up clearly quite inebriated, I laughed along with the other children. This one, however, was a completely different kettle of fish. Yes, he had the heavily made-up face complete with the essential exaggerated, bright red smile. Yes, he had the hugely oversized, brightly coloured garb and yes, he had the massively elongated shoes. Had he been real, he wouldn't have bothered me at all, but he wasn't. He was a mannequin. I held back while my mum and dad followed Tom.

Delighted, he had found a slot to insert a coin and was holding out his hand, determined to see what would happen. When the coin dropped in and the clown began to writhe with laughter, I wanted to run away, but I couldn't. Like in horror films, when the protagonist is absolutely panic-stricken, I was rooted to the ground. My mum assumed I was ill from all the candyfloss I had greedily gobbled. My face was pale, my body covered in goose bumps. Then we were walking away from the awful clown and I was fine again. I didn't even bother to explain. Tom had my hand and was dragging me toward a spaceship ride that spun round and round.

Towards the end of our day at The Pleasure Beach, our parents felt compelled to ensure we had been on every single ride we met the height restriction for, probably so they would never have to return! In the small children's area, a small train ride was tucked away in the corner. Even thinking about it now, as a nearly thirty-year-old woman, I can feel shivers traveling up and down my back as I picture how it looked to an eight-year-old child. It's not there anymore, so I can't prove that there was anything particularly menacing about the appearance of the ride, but I didn't want to go on it. Tom, however, was ecstatic at the thought of riding a miniaturised train round a track and into a dark mine. My mum's expression told me that she would be disappointed if I didn't accompany him, so I did.

I had been on the Big Dipper and ridden the fast carousel without any anxiety whatsoever, but when we entered that mine, terror filled me from head to toe. I gripped the rail in front of us for dear life while we traveled at three miles an hour past a donsey (yes, that actually is the correct term—I didn't just invent it; I'm not that creative) of gnomes who moved back and forth, hacking at the multi-coloured walls with their picks. Their friendly, unchanging expressions did nothing to make me feel welcome. The little things disgusted me. I was petrified that they would do something they shouldn't be able to do. What if one of them was to stop moving as it was programmed, liberate itself from the stand that positioned it, and walk toward me? We came out and again met the bright sky, and I was full of relief.

When the train continued past my waving parents and headed once again for the mouth of the mine, I started to howl. Of course, at the time, I was unable to explain to my parents just what had scared me, exactly. It didn't make sense that I was scared of moving gnomes when my brother was absolutely fine. There was simply no logic behind it.

After that day, I had nightmares for weeks. Every night, I would find myself trapped in that mystic mine, surrounded by gnomes that were perpetually digging away, making no progress, yet smiling inanely.

As I grew up, I slowly began to link the things that scared me, and they all had something in common. They were all made in the image of something that could be alive. The fear was made worse if they were able to move, but the old-fashioned mannequins used in one of the most fashionable retro boutiques scared me with the thought that they might move at some point. This meant that I would hover on the sidelines while my friends rummaged around finding themselves bargains, usually teasing me about my odd phobia. This part of my phobia is called *pediophobia,* which means a fear of dolls. For me, that isn't fully an apt definition, as I was devoted to my Tiny Tears dolls and my Barbies. The porcelain doll bought for me by my grandmother had to stay in the cupboard while I slept, though, and even then, I would struggle to fall asleep worrying that it might make its way out in the dark.

Apparently, *pediophobia* is not that rare. Lots of people are frightened by porcelain dolls and similar things. However, *Automatonophobia* is far more unusual, but it is linked. As an adult, I am now much better at describing what frightens me, and I can evaluate my response, then decide how to deal with it. I am scared of things that are created to look like living things, especially those that have been given the ability to move by animatronics or mechanical systems. They terrify me.

Whilst on holiday in Tenerife with a large group of people, I saw a display designed to welcome guests into the hotel dining area. This was comprised of three huge gorillas that would dance and play instruments to a tune when people walked past. My two little boys thought this was amazing and were immediately drawn to the spectacle. I, on the other hand, stood with my back firmly against the wall, taking deep breaths while shivers of panic ran all over my body. Most people who saw me found this quite amusing, but for me, it was genuinely terrifying. Toward the end of the week, I found that I was more confident walking past the gorillas, but I still had to be at a distance to pass them.

I tried to explain the fear to my friends, who had already accepted that I was a little bit quirky and odd a long time ago! My fear isn't that the figures will come alive, hunt me down, and murder me, *Child's Play* style; it is more that an animatronic will do something that its mechanics should not be allowing it to.

What if the laughing clown at Blackpool Pleasure Beach had stood up in its glass cage or those mining gnomes had started moving away from the spot that they were attached to? In that case, they would be able to do anything that they wanted to. The thought that they could become aggressive and attack me is terrifying, but I find it equally disturbing simply that they might break away from their programming and perform a non-threatening action. This would then mean that anything was possible and all the laws of physics had been broken.

In the film *Big*, Tom Hanks makes a wish on a fortuneteller machine and, while I love that film, that part makes me feel physically sick. It is a machine created in the image of a woman, yet it is able to do things that it has not been designed to do; in this case, it causes the small boy to wake up and find himself in the form of a grown man.

That's another dimension to my fear. If these things suddenly are able to perform actions that are not part of their programming, where is the rational thought behind their action coming from? I'm not particularly religious, but I do believe that when a human being is created, a soul is given to them, which allows them to have conscious free will; they are sentient. An animatronic is not, yet can look and move just like someone who is, and that scares me out of my wits!

I know it is completely irrational. I have never encountered any animatronics that have ever performed in a way they weren't programmed to, apart from in films. Even more ironically, *Mannequin,* an eighties film starring Kim Cattrall, is one of my favourite films. I can explain myself here, though, and make perfect sense to myself, and probably myself alone. The mannequin that comes alive becomes flesh and blood. If good old Kimmy stayed plastic and moved in a disjointed way, adorned with a blank, unchanging expression, the romantic comedy would suddenly become a hide-behind-the-sofa horror film for me.

There are loads of films that try to play on a fear of technology and automatons, *I, Robot* being a famous one. This is a wonderful film and I wouldn't want to take away from the message that we should only rely on technology to a certain extent, as they will never (hopefully!) be given the quality of emotional intelligence, but for a person who should be covering her eyes whilst watching it, I was simply able to enjoy it. This is simply because the robots do not look like any existing life form I am aware of. If they were all given human features, including hair and expressions, they would have scared me half to death.

Luckily for me, I can avoid my phobia, unlike my mother-in-law who is terrified of spiders, which in turn seem to feel the need to visit her frequently. I could simply avoid places where there are likely to be animatronics; theme parks, museums, and festivals are all places that are inessential to my life. But, having two young boys, I am determined not to pass my phobia on to them and as quite a stubborn person, I am also reluctant to let my phobia decide where I can or can't go.

Last Christmas, my husband and I took our sons to Disneyland in Paris. My mother also came with us. We all had our list of things to do over the three days that we would be visiting. My husband wanted to see the fireworks display. My eldest son wanted to go on the Buzz Lightyear ride and shoot aliens. You'd think a problem might arise here, but the aliens look like nothing that I have ever seen alive, and statues of cartoon characters don't bother me in the slightest. I even got under Sulley's arm for a photo! My youngest wanted to see the parade; people in suits are fine. They can do what they want because there aren't any mechanics telling them what they can do. The problem came when my mother started quoting her friends who had raved about how beautiful the It's A Small World ride was. "You get to see all the different parts of the world," she said. "All the festivals are displayed, like Diwali and Christmas being celebrated. We will sail around in a little boat. You'll love it!"

I didn't love it. I loathed it. It was my very definition of Hell on Earth. We went round at a stupidly slow pace past a plethora of miniature people all moving in different ways. There were Spanish senoritas dancing in the same movement endlessly. There were children stuck in a state of laughter, going round and round on a carousel. This also scares me. Irrationally, I can't help but think, what if they are aware of what they are doing and are stuck repeating the same action? It went on and on. My heart raced, my palms sweated, and yet I was shivering.

"Oh, I didn't think about that. You hate these things, don't you," was my mother's response!

When we finally emerged back into the sunlight, all I could think about was getting off the boat before it started to go round again and I was trapped. Combined with the boat shaking under our moving weight and my unsteady legs, it was no wonder that I stumbled less than gracefully out of the boat. My mother was still in a dream world, reliving the ride, while I was hoping that I would be able to sleep without seeing their painted faces in my dreams. We went for a walk to the Alice in Wonderland maze, with the aim of settling my nerves. Just as I was starting to settle down and focus in on the beautiful flowers decorating the area, my mother made the mistake of increasing my anxiety to a whole new level

"I just don't understand why they bother you so much. I mean, if it was like the middle of the night and you were stuck in there, I could imagine that would be scary."

That was the point when I stood in the middle of Disneyland, at twenty-nine years old, and had to wipe tears of terror off my cheeks.

On a normal day, my phobia affects me very little, though, and for this, I am grateful. Even living in a tourist town, I can make the choice to avoid coming into contact with any animatronics. When I am put in a new situation, like going for a job interview or having to meet new people, this can also cause me to panic. I know that many people experience some anxiety in new situations, but it isn't a fear of embarrassing myself or failing in some way that bothers me; it's the experience of meeting new people whom I may not be able to read. I find myself unnerved by people who have unreadable expressions. This could be someone who stares blankly at me or who remains silent when I would expect them to say something. They remind me of automatons, because they don't behave in a manner that is "typically human." As a teacher, I often have blank little faces staring up at me and usually I can attribute an emotion to each one; perhaps they are confused, bored, half-asleep...

Plus, I can usually have an effect on that expression by telling a bad joke or asking them a question to check that they are following the lesson. If they all continued to look at me with completely blank expressions, which has happened before in my nightmares, I would probably fall to pieces.

As a supposedly intelligent person, I have thought about ways to conquer my fear. Having mild OCD, which I am medicated for on and off already, I have discussed cognitive-behavioural therapy with my doctor to tackle both this and the phobia, but the idea of having somebody actually change my emotional responses to something scares me out as well! I don't like the thought of anybody messing with my mind or altering who I am, even though I do believe that I am the product of my surroundings and not a finished product. Despite this, I still like to believe that I am in control.

Desensitisation certainly hasn't worked! I know that some would argue that perhaps I would need to be stuck in a room with the very thing that scares me until I became so used to it being there, it wouldn't bother me anymore. Based on the fact that just typing that last sentence has caused my heart rate to increase, I would be worried that my heart may not be able to sustain the increased rate. I would either suffer a heart attack or end up having to be detained in a psychiatric unit for the rest of my life as a result.

The only method of combating the fear that I have found works is breathing exercises. Some doctors believe relaxation exercises are the best way to deal with a phobia such as mine. I would agree. Deep breaths and focusing on something else, such as imagining myself sunbathing on a beach far away from wherever I am at the time, certainly helps. However, I admit that this isn't really dealing with the fear. It is more a way of avoiding it and helping the exposure to pass more pleasantly. Should the fear ever escalate to the point where I could not deal with it, or perhaps with the world ever becoming a more technological place, animatronics might become something that I would have to deal with on a daily basis, and I would definitely try other methods of coping.

I am aware there are medications that can help, and I would accept cognitive-behavioural therapy. This is something I will always have to live with, but I'm not prepared to let it affect me in a detrimental way. On the plus side, my children think it's absolutely hilarious.

STACKING BLOCKS

Angie Orenstein

Even though it was almost thirty years ago, I still remember the event like it was just yesterday. I was twelve and in sixth grade when the mime came to our school.

Kids always get excited when there's a school assembly of any kind because it means getting out of classes for a while. So, like all the other kids, I was happy that day to be heading to the auditorium to see a silent clown performing tricks. The entire school was there—sixth, seventh, and eighth graders—and to make things even better, when my class filed in, we happened to be directed into the very first row. We plopped down cross-legged on the gymnasium floor as the roar of 300 preteens' constant chatter slowly fizzled out and the show began.

I clapped and laughed along with the other kids as the white-faced mime ran around juggling colorful balls and acting out humorous scenarios. Suddenly, he stepped to the first row and thrust his hand toward the girl sitting next to me, gesturing that he wanted her to stand up and join him. Like most middle-schoolers would, she giggled and vigorously shook her head *no*. Then he turned his attention to me.

Now, before I continue, you have to understand: I was painfully shy. I never raised my hand in class to answer a question. In fact, I could not get out of my seat to walk across the room in front of others. Let me give you an example.

Years later, as a sophomore in high school, I had one of my commonly occurring migraine headaches, so I popped an aspirin into my mouth in the middle of science class, then realized I didn't have any water with me. As the bitter pill began to melt in my mouth, I ached to raise my hand and ask the teacher if I could go to the bathroom, but I remained silent and glued to my seat. The idea of eyes following me and ears hanging on my every word instantly froze my blood with irrational fear.

I don't know why I was like that. It's inexplicable. Might as well call it what it is—a phobia.

Back to sixth grade… As the mime reached his black and white striped arm toward me, I mimicked what the girl next to me did. I mean, it worked for her, right? I smiled and shook my head *no*. For some reason—a reason I will never understand—he did not go away, like he did with the girl next to me. Maybe he felt he was running out of time, maybe he felt I was an easy target (I was about sixty-five pounds soaking wet, and the girl next to me looked to be twice my size.) Regardless, he would not take no for an answer. He grasped my hand and pulled me across the waxed gymnasium floor.

Horrified is the only word that comes to mind as to how I felt having my skinny ass dragged out in front for all to see. Laughter erupted and I had no choice but to rise to my feet on a pair of shaky, skinny legs.

My heart was beating fast, a thin sheen of sweat had broken out all over my body, and the people around me were nothing but blurs. I think the low hum deep in my ears was warning me that I could possibly faint from fear.

The mime picked up a square blue block, made eye contact with me, then pointed his chin toward a pile of identical blocks. He was indicating that I should pick one up and place it on top of the block in his hands. What choice did I have? Moving like a stiff robot walking underwater, I did as I was told. He continued to gesture toward the blocks. Once they were stacked a good six or seven blocks high, and I was thinking I might soon be able to escape back to my seat on the floor, the unthinkable happened. He purposely dropped the bottom one to the floor, then indicated it with that pointy white chin of his.

Mortified, I bent down to pick it up, and he immediately popped the top one off the stack and it landed on the floor. I picked that one up, and as I was placing it back on top, he again dropped one from the bottom. Like a fool, I continued to pick up dropped blocks and place them back on to his stack while waves of laughter from hundreds of students crashed over me. I was drowning in humiliation.

That day stayed strong in my memory for years to come. I avoided situations where I had to speak to groups of people or even walk across a crowded room. Sometimes these moments were unavoidable, and during those times, my chest felt heavy, I broke into a cold sweat, and felt dizzy as the room slowly tipped on its side.

I slunk through high school, staying quiet and under the radar, avoiding most social situations as much as possible, other than quiet get-togethers and excursions with my family and close friends. I was always fine one on one, or in small groups. I laughed and joked and enjoyed normal activities and a normal life, as long as I didn't have to face a crowd.

I went to college at a very small school and I think this helped me, too, because most of my classes consisted of a mere handful of people. I started becoming more comfortable as I got to know my fellow classmates. I was even able to read a few stories out loud to the six people in my creative writing class. In one class, we were assigned to pick a topic and write a magazine article about it. I put some real thought into it before I chose shyness and entitled my story *Silence Can Be Golden*. I did some research and was shocked to discover that some very famous actors, like Johnny Carson, were so painfully shy they often threw up before appearing before an audience. The King of Late Night Comedy actually puking because he was afraid to walk on stage? This thought offered me hope!

Since my college major was communications and I wanted to be a journalist, it followed logically that I needed to interview people to write stories. I didn't like that, but I did it, and each time I did, interviewing got just a tiny bit easier. By senior year, I was editor of my college newspaper. My good friend in college, Donna, asked me to be a bridesmaid in her wedding. I accepted, put on the velvety gown and walked down the aisle with all eyes on me. Sure, I felt like I was going to faint, but I didn't...and I realized, *hey, I can do this.*

For those facing the same phobia as I do, I wish I could tell you about a specific turning point in my life that changed me from painfully shy to aggressively outgoing, but that's not the case. Not only is there not a specific event that made me turn the corner, but I have not become aggressively outgoing. I have, however, changed drastically...for the better, I might add! And if you ask me to tell you how, I can say only two words—age and experience.

As the years went on, I continually found myself in situations where I had to talk to people and face my fears. I went on job interviews. I went to weddings and parties. I dated. I met my husband. I met new friends, some of them pretty outgoing. Soon, they started taking me to karaoke.

The first time I went to karaoke was with my sister and a friend of hers, probably a good fifteen years ago. I remember saying, "I'll go but I won't sing!"

That night was a lot of fun and I found myself wanting to sing. I was scared, so I went up to sing with my sister and friend. Being up there with two other people was still a nerve-wracking experience, but it was a rush and, as I walked back to my seat, heart pounding in my chest, I found myself pretty proud for confronting my fears head-on. My sister's friend hugged me and said how great it was that I went up there but, she added, "The only way to really lose your karaoke virginity is to sing alone."

"Never!" I gasped at the very idea.

Yet, a few months later, back at the karaoke bar—and without any alcohol, I might add—I was up there singing alone: *Head Over Feet* by Alanis Morissette. I'm surprising myself right now by remembering that.

Now, my husband and I go to karaoke every week. We have a large group of friends who we know from karaoke and other places in our lives, too. For instance, I met many great friends through the Moms & Tots group I joined with my baby daughter, who is now fourteen.

I think the key to any fear or phobia is to confront it as much as possible. If it's just swept under the rug and avoided, that can be a temporary fix, a bandage of sorts, but someday, it will slide back out and you'll be forced to deal with it. By confronting your fears gradually, one baby step at a time, you'll slowly get it under control. I think it will always be there, but it will be something manageable. It's kind of like stacking those frustrating blocks that mime had. You just have to keep bending down, picking them up, and putting them back on, even though they keep dropping off again.

Even though I do karaoke on a regular basis, I am sometimes surprised when my old phobia rears its ugly head. I see it once in a while when I'm at work. I'm a writer for my local town newspaper. Every week, I contact new people whom I've never spoke with and set up interviews with them. I'm pretty good with one on one, face to face, but sometimes I am asked to cover a big event in a room filled with many people. As I walk across the crowded room or hall, I feel the weight of many strange eyes upon me and my heart rate speeds up just a bit. I take a breath, swallow that hard knot of fear in my throat, and shake myself out of it—smiling and extending my hand, introducing myself to the new face in front of me. I'm always fine, just as long as that face is not covered in white paint!

"The wise man in the storm prays to God, not for safety from danger, but for deliverance from fear. It is the storm within that endangers him, not the storm without."
Ralph Waldo Emerson

PHOBIAS SPROUTING FROM SEEDS OF FEAR

Toianna Wika

Since childhood, anxiety has been my *modus operandi,* because I never felt safe and feared for my survival. I barely dared to breathe and learned how to be invisible around my violent, alcoholic father, who self-medicated with drugs of all kinds for his bipolar disorder. Most of my energy went into blending into the walls and camouflaging myself, and freezing in silence, my best chance for survival at the time. The only kind of dependability I knew was the next crisis, having to try to predict the severity, and deciding my strategy for how to survive.

Rarely did I have basic needs met. Oftentimes, I did not have enough to eat or was not warm enough. My mother and I made a lifestyle of tiptoeing through blood, vomit, and broken glass as quietly as possible. I went to bed hungry oftentimes, because crisis was the routine, rather than eating and bathing. I remember shivering in my bed and watching snow blow inside, after my father tore off the front door in a rage. My father brought strangers home from downtown bars to stay with us, sometimes for months. Frequently, my father forced me and my mother to stay awake nights and listen to his ramblings about his rotten childhood. He broke bottles over my mother's head, dragged her around the house by her hair, and shot guns over our heads. He took drugs that made him hallucinate, thinking we were in a war and needed to get guns to protect ourselves, or he slept for days without waking, or he awoke thinking I was a waitress somewhere in Asia.

I regarded my father as a monster and cringed in his presence most of the time. I remained as invisible as possible, by barely breathing. On weekends, I hid from him in the neighborhood, while my mother was at work and I was left in his care. My father beat and raped my mother in front of me. He threw my grandfather into kitchen cabinets, which broke his hip one Thanksgiving. We learned to dread holidays, which seemed to incite the most violence. He threatened to cut off my mother's toes and oftentimes had a knife to my mother's throat when I left for school. I did not know whether or not my mother would be alive when I returned home.

My childhood was a series of situations that bred anxiety, and the situations became so routine that they became normal to me. This led to the fact that I filter and experience reality differently than so-called *normal* people, which makes life challenging, mostly because my differences make communication with others difficult and exhausting at best, other times impossible, unbearable.

My husband and children affectionately call me Melvin, after my male equivalent, the protagonist in the movie *As Good As It Gets.* Humor has been incredibly medicinal. Calling me Melvin has served as a signal between us, also, for times when I am getting too wound up in some social situation.

I believe that my phobias have sprouted out of seeds of fear, planted during my childhood. I have come to understand my fears in terms of intensity and to regard my phobias in terms of circumstantial triggers that exacerbate my fears to the point of my becoming frozen in place, like the proverbial deer in headlights. My phobias are like fears pressed into a book, or stamped and ground into me by a boot. They are fears with exclamation points.

Through the years, acquaintances, friends, school peers, and coworkers have remarked impatiently to me to "Stop being so sensitive!" and "You're making a big deal out of nothing," with the tone of *just stop doing it*, insinuating that I want to lose sleep, suffer, and feel weird, alone, separated from others, with abnormal reactions simply to get attention.

Many said I was looking for them to be my protector. It was like I had a chill that I could not shake and wanted to hold onto others for warmth, but it was not the cold, and I felt the need for a protector years after there was any *real* threat to my safety.

Lack of understanding and empathy from others has led me to commiserate with poet Charles Bukowski, who, when asked if he hated people, replied, "I like people... (but) just seem to feel better when they aren't around."

In my twenties, I worked with a psychotherapist who told me I was like a war veteran who returns home without legs. He helped me to accept that my scars will not go away, but also to discover ways to work around them. He diagnosed me a couple of decades ago with Generalized Anxiety Disorder (GAD), but through the years I have sampled a smorgasbord of anxiety-related disorders, such as post-traumatic stress disorder (PTSD), obsessive-compulsive disorder (OCD), panic with agoraphobia, and a variety of *specific phobias* as described in the *DSM IV-TR*. Also, I have dealt with paranoia and a milder form of bipolar disorder called *cyclothymia*.

When I was seeing my therapist, I remember drinking alcohol to numb myself as he probed deeper and began tweaking nerves. At that time, I suffered mostly from *agliophobia* (fear of pain) and *dementophobia* (fear of becoming insane). I was too afraid to find out what might happen if I let myself feel my feelings about my childhood, and I was terrified that I was going insane, like my father. I had been drinking heavily by that time and did not realize that my insanity was the result of alcoholic behavior, like my father.

Fear of darkness, the first phobia I ever had, has haunted me most and impacted my life most significantly, after fear of pain and insanity, and accounts, no doubt, for my fear of change and the unknown. Extreme fear of darkness began the night my father locked me outside purposefully, when I was five years old. He thought it would be amusing to see what I would do when he imitated the voice he knew scared me from the radio program *The Shadow Knows*. I cried, begged, and clawed at the door to get inside, but he forced me to stay outside in the dark for what felt like hours.

Decades later, on nights that I am exhausted or stressed, my fear of darkness peaks. I lie awake, barely able to breathe, and certainly do not open my eyes. I *know* there is a grinning monster face an inch from mine, just waiting. When I hear the house creak, I know it is the monsters, reminding me they are there, waiting for the perfect moment to pounce.

There has been an interesting relationship for me through the years between my *nyctophobia* (fear of darkness) and *teratophobia* (fear of monsters), and my obsession with horror movies.

I am religious and have been soothed by accounts of saints who have dealt with darkness and demons. A large part of me trusts God to protect me, while reasoning tells me the monsters do not exist. Yet, reasoning does not necessarily extinguish the irrational. I have the deep-seated belief I share with no one that monsters really are crouched outside of the windows and are waiting for the perfect time to get me. This has led to an obsession of watching horror movies to scare myself, then daring myself to walk by windows at night or going to the basement alone.

To avoid sleepless nights, I trim unnecessary stress and try to stay on top of getting enough rest. I get my husband to give me a massage, or leave lights on those nights I realize too late that I did not take adequate preventive care.

I have been afraid of deep water, like swimming in lakes, where I cannot see to the bottom. I have been afraid of great white sharks since seeing *Jaws,* and having to scramble out of swimming pools when imagining the light underwater on the wall of the pool was the side of a boat. My heart palpitated because I felt for sure I would be attacked. This could be related to my fear of the unknown and expecting something awful when I was in middle school and had to be forced to put my hand inside a box to identify by touch what was there. I remember our teacher's astonishment that I feared getting hurt by what was inside. That was one incident where my differences from classmates stood out.

I have an incredible fear of physical pain, and regress to a young child when facing needles and dentists. In fact, I cannot concentrate on anything else a doctor is saying when I know I am awaiting a flu shot or Novocain. I can't look when I get shots, and my kids hold my hand.

As a child, I was forced to have many fillings and at that time, in the nineteen-fifties, dentists were not as hip to psychology. Had they been asked, they probably would have snorted at complaints with a come-back like, "Deal with it." In fairness, however, a dentist would have been forced to read my mind, since I had learned to stuff my feelings to the point that when I was in high school, someone trying to befriend me remarked how odd it was I made no sound when I laughed or cried.

Another kind of fear that has followed me through life has been fear of failure, because teachers flagged me as slow and as special education material in elementary school. I felt humiliated most of the time, too tired to concentrate, frozen in fear while standing alone in front of the class when we had to recite poetry. That is the earliest I remember stage fright and fear of public speaking. Peers began making fun of me once my fifth grade teacher held me back. In high school, I suffered from fear of failure and of success after I fought the system and proved that I could do above average work. And I had a fear of receiving praise, as though someone praising me were burning me or slugging me.

Decades later, living in my skin with these issues, I still blame myself for my differences from *normal* people and start beating myself up emotionally, which leads to overeating and other self-destructive thoughts, feelings, and actions, if I do not consciously play enough of the movie reel of my childhood in my mind. I do not blame anyone else, aside from circumstances occurring in my childhood because of coping skills my parents chose.

As an adult, I realize I am responsible for responses and actions, and have learned to remind myself that, like the war veteran who awakes disoriented and has to readjust constantly to the shift in reality of having no legs, I am *different,* too. It is not my fault that I cannot rely on my instincts of knowing how to react appropriately when I am upset by a person or situation, although I am accountable for compensating the best that I can with tools I have learned.

I do constant *reality checks,* by trying not to react to a situation that bothers me until I have reminded myself about how thin-skinned I am, prone to overreacting, and that my interpretation of a given situation is probably distorted, as I never learned how *normal* people would react in like circumstances. My frame of reference is *different*. So, I run any troublesome situations and feelings I have by family and friends I trust.

Common sense and life experience have shown me that I cannot altogether obliterate fears from childhood of how I view myself and others, and how I cope. However, my desire to help myself and to succeed has helped more than traditional therapy, and more than I ever learned from reading or even working as a mental health specialist.

In particular, my years training as a Mary Kay beauty consultant helped immensely because success in business is commensurate with self-confidence. Surprisingly, I was attracted to the positive "Rah, rah!" of our team and our phenomenally charismatic director, with whom we met collectively each week. Our director taught us sales skills, but more importantly, how to be positive and set the example of building an invisible fence against negativity.

Through our sales director, we were introduced to an abundance coach who taught us to the concept that how we think significantly affects how we feel, which in turn affects our choices and action, and finally, the results we get. The focus of our energy determines our reality.

Through a variety of in-class exercises, our coach demonstrated tools for gaining perspective and generating positive energy. An example of our coach's focus on energy is twentieth-century sociologist Robert K. Merton's self-fulfilling prophecy, which leads to *"Our material reality is the reflection of where we primarily focus our energy."*

My paralyzing fear of speaking in front of a handful of women cost me success with Mary Kay. Of course, I had a fear of women, too. I had experienced them as cruel, deceptive, and catty until I joined Mary Kay and, incidentally, worked through some of my issues with women, especially attractive and "girly" women who know how to accessorize and, like artists, work miracles with cosmetics. I realize that, to some extent, how I viewed women was the distorted reflection of myself and a distorted interpretation of their words and actions.

However, my dream was not to become a Mary Kay director, but to return to my childhood dream of writing. Supposing I am successful as a writer and public appearances become necessary, I will decide at that time what to do.

Most situations elicit fear from me to start, which sometimes I can set aside and sometimes not.

I have been afraid for years of being made fun of and criticized for my weight and the way I dress. I am afraid others will notice I am *different*. I fear embarrassing my family with my eccentricities and lack of conventional social skills. I do not like trying to pretend I am normal during the few occasions I do go out, rather than feeling free to be accepted as my beatnik self.

I have fear of grocery shopping because of constant near-collisions with grocery carts and people not ever using manners. So, I try to shop off hours. I avoid malls at Christmas and during big sales, to avoid possible panic attacks or aggressive reactions when shoppers bump and shove one another, especially close to Christmas. I walk past groups of people with my arms clenched, so it will not hurt me if they bump me. Shopping of any kind on Black Friday is out of the question.

My first memory of a nightmare is having crawled into a tight space under a chair to hide from a bear chasing me. That is what I associate with my first memory of claustrophobia.

One Fourth of July, I went to Gasworks Park in Seattle to hear the Philharmonic Orchestra violin concertos and to hear Robert Fulghum speak. I found myself squished into a sardine can, with no room to breathe. There was no way to leave, had I wanted. That left a scar and made me reluctant ever to go into large crowds. That, and the fact that I waited all night in line once to get a free piano and had people shove me to the floor and trample me, added significantly to my fear of safety in a crowd.

I have witnessed individuals yelling and being escorted out of stores by security. We are on welfare, and my husband and I start our trek to food pantry shelves by taking the bus, where young people look at us as though they are daring us to ask for seats reserved for older and disabled individuals. Sometimes I have the courage for me, but always for my husband. Many turn my request into a racial issue.

Meanwhile, I cannot help but face constantly being treated differently because of our lack of money. People treat us like we are slow, stupid, pitiable, and lazy. I am humiliated asking for help and aware of politicians comparing the poor to raccoons and stray animals.

We have no choice, at least once a month, to head to first come, first served, dog-eat-dog lines to wait two hours to get inside the door and wait for another hour, with people who make sure we know how much they resent that we are first and infer they resent how much we fill our cart. Coupled with ongoing background panic of not finding a job and getting older, I feel certain that accounts for my deteriorating health, including more instances of hyperventilating and panic attacks.

This and experiences with the quality of life controversy over individuals like our son account for my having developed a social phobia that has turned into agoraphobia. Rarely do I leave the house anymore.

Self-awareness of feeling hungry, angry, sickly, or tired is vital. I have learned that a balance between ruthless honesty with myself and kindness toward myself is important. The more nurturing and tuned in I am with how I feel physically, mentally, and emotionally, the more likely I am to choose wisely regarding what I need and what I can handle. Or if I need to handle something I know will be difficult, I know to prepare accordingly. Maintaining a positive focus is my second most important task. Doing reality checks is third. Running potential scenarios by others, whom I trust to know me, helps when I need to go to a gathering—for example, our daughter's upcoming high school graduation. And I take along a friend or my family for support. Fourthly, I have to remind myself to take a breath and not react too quickly, if something happens that trips my alarms.

In the past year, when my physical health problems, like blood pressure, started becoming affected by emotional stress, I began taking the mood stabilizer Citalopram.

Mostly, I have filed my fears away in three categories: those that are daily issues, like general anxiety; those that are situational and less frequent; and phobias, the least frequent, probably because I avoid situations where they are likely to crop up.

I socialize selectively and do not talk to many people I do not know, which works since my husband loves to talk to everyone. I avoid situations and people I know will stir up conflict. Regardless of how anyone tries to minimize my feelings, these days I try listening to myself about what I need, if it isn't too outrageous and does not involve telling others off. I have learned through the years that I do not have to beat myself up for my limitations or practice being my own worst enemy. I am learning to become my own best advocate, protector, and friend.

SHARK BAIT

David Price

The first phobia I ever experienced was caused by a movie. I've been searching for a name for this phobia, but I can't find the exact right one. So, let's call it, "Scary-things-live-under-the-water-and-want-to-eat-me-phobia." I imagine you can figure out the movie based on the phobia, right? That movie is, of course, *Jaws*.

I saw *Jaws* at the theater when I was eight. Now, I was already watching all those great Universal and Hammer horror movies based on Dracula, Frankenstein, the Wolfman, and the Mummy, and Japanese monster movies like Godzilla, every weekend on Creature Feature. Plus, *Jaws* was rated PG, so I'm sure my parents thought I could handle it. Unfortunately, that movie led to an unrelenting fear of swimming in deep water.

I should explain my relationship to the water before *Jaws*. My parents met at a lake in New Hampshire. As soon as possible, my mother had me taking swimming lessons at the YMCA, and later, more advanced lessons at something that was called New England Divers. I have always loved swimming. My brother and I were like fish when we spent summers at the cottage. *Jaws* did a number on that, at least for me.

We had a raft in the lake, which was probably eighty to one hundred feet from shore, depending on the yearly water level of the lake. All the kids have always loved the raft. They swam out there and played king of the raft, cannonballed each other, and chased each other around it.

After seeing *Jaws*, fear would grip me whenever I tried to swim out to the raft, especially if I was by myself. I would find myself swimming as quickly as possible, and I would be completely exhausted by the time I reached the raft. If I remember correctly, there were even occasions when people had to come from the raft and swim back out with me. I was too scared to do it by myself. Getting back was no easier. I know there were at least a few times when I begged for someone to come and pick me up in a canoe.

One time, we went to visit friends at Sebago Lake, in Maine. I had never been there before and this unfamiliarity made the fear even worse. We were playing in the water with some other kids our age, and there was this rock we could jump off, into the water. It was probably about fifteen feet high or so, good enough for a thrill. I remember jumping off and swimming back to the shore to do it again. Suddenly, something *huge* swam right underneath me, scraping my body as it passed. I am not sure if I screamed, or gasped, or whatever, but I knew the other kids were looking at me. I was terrified. A shark had just swum right underneath me and would be turning around any second to finish me off. Of course, instead of a great white shark swimming under me in a lake in Maine, what had really happened was I had swum over a large rock that was close to the surface. I swam past it; nothing swam past me. In my mind, though, if only for a few moments, it was a shark, no doubt about it.

I managed to deal with the fear eventually; although I think there were a few years after that when I did not spend a lot of time swimming in the lake. I may have gone out in the canoe, or wading up to my waist, but not too much swimming out to the raft. At the age of fourteen, I started reading Stephen King. He instantly became my favorite author and I read everything by Stephen King that I could get my hands on. When I was sixteen, his short story *The Raft* was published in *Twilight Zone* magazine.

Naturally, I purchased a copy and read it. I loved that story; it really scared the hell out of me. I also believed it kind of added salt to the wound of a phobia that I was coping with at the time.

So, while I may have been dealing with my fear of sharks and rationalizing the fact that they do not live in fresh water, this other story came along and introduced me to some random slime monster that can completely ruin a swimming hole experience. I have always had an over-active imagination, and I think *The Raft* just piled on to that already-existing phobia. There went another year that I barely went into the lake.

Probably a year or two after reading *The Raft,* my cousins from Colorado came up to the lake cottage with us. These guys were definitely on the more adventurous side and loved to do all things outdoorsy. I think they knew about my fear of swimming in the deeper water, even though they never said anything to me. They tried to convince me to swim around the lake with them. There was no way I was going to do that, uh-uh. I was a strong enough swimmer, sure, but I was not going to just offer myself up to those dark, underwater beasties as bait. I mean, how stupid did they think I was? So they went without me.

And guess what? Surprise, surprise, they actually came back just fine! Okay, now we were up there for a whole week together and they were going to do this around-the-lake swim every day. After a few days, I gave in and went with them. Was I scared? You bet. Were all these scary things swimming underneath me, just waiting for the perfect moment to strike? I was sure of it. But I stayed with them and made it around the lake and back alive. The second time was a little easier, and the third time even easier than that. Overall, I was starting to realize there was probably nothing in the lake that wanted to eat me. Even if there was something big enough down there, it had its chance and passed on me. Swimming in the lake became easier, and although I won't say the fear has ever completely subsided, it is really just this tingling in the back of my head now. I can just push it away if it starts to come to the forefront. Occasionally, I will go tubing on the lake. This year, my brother and I even swam around the lake with our kids.

Now, the ocean is a different story. Even though the fear brought on by *Jaws* and *The Raft* had merged at some point, it seemed that I had to deal with them separately, in the lake and in the ocean. I will say, even though I dealt with my fear up at the lake for many years, I completely avoided the ocean for more than a decade. My first snorkeling experience was in Cancun at the age of twenty-three or so. There is this lagoon called Xel-Há that serves as a natural aquarium for the tropical fish down there. It was awesome! I was nervous, but the lagoon gets no deeper than eight feet. The tropical fish were everywhere, and they were so beautiful. Schools of these fish would swim right up to and around you. That was just a great experience for me. We did a little more snorkeling near our hotel, but never in any really deep water.

My wife and I went to Aruba on our honeymoon a couple of years later. They have this shipwreck down there that tourists can snorkel. It is pretty deep, and a boat has to take you out to it. I had loved snorkeling in Cancun, so I worked up the courage to snorkel the shipwreck. That was another great time for me. The water was so clear, and we could see so far down. When I snorkeled it, there were scuba divers down there swimming amongst the shipwreck. There were also these big fish down there with them, about the same size as a man, say five feet long or so. I think they might have been barracuda, but I'm not sure. To see these big fish and people swimming around each other was something new to me. I was fascinated and forgot all about my fear of deep water while I was out there.

Years later, my wife and I took a cruise with our kids through the Caribbean. One of the stops was the Grand Caymans and we took a boat out a couple miles to some place called Stingray City. This is a sandbar quite a way from shore where the stingrays hang out by the dozens. They seem to be tame, and swimmers can even feed them right out of their hands. One girl rubbed her hand on her stomach after feeding some fish to a stingray, and another came over and sucked on her belly, where she had rubbed. She was freaked out at first, but then said it just tickled. It was weird, but harmless.

On that same cruise, I also managed to go parasailing at one of the stops. I was the second guy to sign up for it. The first guy was really nervous, I guess, and they only put him up there about fifteen feet or so. Well, apparently my wife had told the crew that I was really gung-ho, or something like that. They put me up so high; I was like a human kite. From my vantage point, the boat that was pulling me looked to be about the size of a matchbox car. It was awesome, to see the beautiful Caribbean waters from up there. Everything is so clean and clear, not like the ocean up in New England. Seeing the ocean like that, in all its crystal clear beauty, you just want to be in it, soaking in the experience.

So that's it; that is how I have dealt with my phobia, one piece at a time. While I can't say it has ever completely vanished, I have managed to confront it and the fear has lessened considerably. I think that is probably the best way to deal with any fear, face it and come away stronger. Every time you face one of those irrational fears and survive them, it loosens its grip on you just a little bit. Eventually, if you can expose yourself to your phobia enough, I suspect it probably fades away completely.

SNAKES ALIVE!

Kim Curley

If I had my choice of locations to live on this planet, I'd move to Ireland. The attraction for most people would be the green isle's beautiful landscapes and rich cultural heritage. Those are just two of the perks. But, for me, I'd enjoy living in a place free from snakes.

I was raised to live in fear of snakes. In the state I grew up in, over thirty species of snakes slithered and slinked around. Within those varieties, four venomous snakes dwelled as well: cottonmouth, copperhead, eastern massasauga, and timber rattlesnake. These species are part of the pit viper family of snakes. The heat-sensing pits near their elliptical eyes give the ominous glare that screams, "Leave me alone or you're going to get hurt."

In my opinion, all snakes have that same nasty glower.

I realize there are beneficial snakes working to keep down rodent and insect populations. However, when I see a slithering, creeping snake, I perceive them to be evil. When I've been unfortunate enough to see a snake, I get panic attacks, my heart pounds, and my chest tightens up. Instead of being calm and slowly turning away, I make eye contact with the creatures, frozen in place, unsure of my best escape route away from those slippery ropes. Even the slightest glimpse of a picture of a snake makes me shiver and I get goose bump flesh. My condition is called ophidiophobia, an abnormal fear of snakes.

My parents were a major influence on my perception of snakes, especially my mother. They regaled me with numerous, frightening encounters with poisonous snakes, which were enough to convince me that I never, ever wanted to be near the reptiles.

Our family lived in an area surrounded by creeks, streams, and canals. Fishing wasn't just a pastime; it was a skill you learned before you could even walk. The entire family helped gather up all the necessary equipment, pack food for the day, and get bait. We either dug up our own night crawlers (earthworms), or we went seining for minnows in the shallow creeks. With the fishing net affixed to two lightweight poles, my father and I watched for any signs of our intended prey. Once we spotted the flashes of silver in the water, we paid close attention to the swim patterns of the minnows. Carefully, we would enter the water, with my father positioned closest to the shore and the bucket for the tiny fish, while I wound up closest to the bank. We dipped the poles in the water, the net ballooning out as we walked toward the school of fish. While I focused on keeping the pole down in the water, my dad would yell at me to watch out for snakes. Holding my breath, I'd stop in my tracks, eyes scanning everywhere, expecting a fanged creature to leap at me from the nooks and crannies of rocks, or holes in the riverbank. If the coast was clear, I'd drop the net and run screaming from the creek. With a firm voice, my father always assured me that he wouldn't let anything bad happen to me. Back into the water I went, along with a firm reminder that the only time I was allowed to drop the net was if a snake was chasing the minnows.

We didn't have any poisonous snakes around our house. With all the fertile land surrounding us, neighbors had silent competitions to see who could grow the most and best food crops. Along with the gardens came the garden-variety snakes. They were good for going after invasive bugs, fighting for the same food supply as the toads.

My least favorite job was pulling weeds between all the rows of carrots, corn, squash, and lettuce. I spent more time circling the plowed patches of garden than the actual weeding. The face of a garden snake isn't as sinister as the pit viper species. Instead of a furrowed brow and stern look, the garden snakes have beady eyes. When coiled on the ground, they look like shiny, black satin ribbons, with blue stripes. I almost always spooked one of these little ribbons out of the area I needed to weed, and I'd watch in fear and awe at the amount of speed this little creature could gain without the use of legs. Anxiety would grip me, and I could feel my entire body freeze in fear. Sick to my stomach, I'd cast more leery glances around, wondering where the next slimy rope lay in wait. Once I'd gained some composure, I'd go running to my mother, whining about seeing a snake in the garden. I would beg and plead with her not to make me go back out to what I perceived as a snake-infested yard. My mother hated snakes more than I did, but even she would make me turn around and face my fear. There was no getting out of weeding the garden for me.

We had friends in the country who shared a spot of their farmland where my parents were allowed to put our family camping trailer. The trailer sat at the top of a bank that led to the canal. The canal system was rich with fishing and hunting. The area was also crawling with snakes. There were rules for me to abide by while we camped. To keep me safe from harm, I was not allowed to go down to the canal alone. Not just because of the fear of drowning, but because of the cottonmouths that liked to warm themselves on the banks, or hide among the reeds and grass going down the bank to the water. My mother told me of a time before I was born when she was readying the boat to fish. The boat was kept on the dock, flipped over so it wouldn't fill with water, should it rain. As she began to pick up the boat, she heard a faint hiss before she saw the cottonmouth coiled and ready to strike. Somehow she got away unscathed, but the memory of the encounter made her shake all over. Whether the story was true or not, it was enough to keep me away from the water and the dock.

Our friends not only shared a spot of land for our trailer, but also generously gave us a small portion of their crop area for us to have a small garden. There was no garden hose that far out, so we filled our water cooler to water the plants. My parents had purchased a kid-sized watering can so that I could help water the garden. At five years of age, I figured out that I was making triple the amount of watering trips as my parents, so I asked if I could go rock hunting on the dirt road.

I agreed to their request to stick to the road, as I had associated the canal with danger, and skipped off in search of pyrite and quartz, with the hopes of finding fossils or arrowheads. I had barely begun when I heard a scream coming from the garden. I saw my mother running out of the field, and my father picked up a large rock and disappeared among the stalks of corn. I ran back to my mom and she kept me from coming nearer. My dad yelled from the depths of the garden to keep our distance when he came out. My mom grabbed me and we backed away from the area, vigilant for any dangers that could be lurking elsewhere. My father walked out carrying a thick branch. Dangling off the far end of the branch was the biggest snake I'd ever seen.

My mother had been weeding and watering when she had stepped on a sleepy cottonmouth sunning itself in the field. We both shook as we watched my dad carry the lifeless form of the snake over to a wooded area and tossed the body. I felt sad for the poor creature for a few seconds, but then I remembered what could have happened if my mom had been bitten. My early childhood years along the canal were some of the best years of my life, and the most terrifying, at the same time.

Years after we got rid of our trailer, my dad took me camping along the river. We set up our simple campsite, which consisted of our sleeping bags and a circle of stones for the campfire pit. I looked forward to sleeping under the starry sky that evening, until it was time to get into the sleeping bag. My father reminded me to beat the sleeping bag and turn it upside-down to insure no snakes had slipped inside. This is not something I wanted to hear just before going to sleep. Needless to say, I spent that night worried more about sneaky-snakes crawling into my sleeping bag than actually sleeping. The next camping trip my dad and I went on, we slept in the back of the station wagon, away from the snakes.

The older I got, the less time I spent going camping and hunting with my dad. This also meant less of a chance for coming across those poisonous ropes I'd spent so much time avoiding most of my life.

When I became old enough to drive, cruising in my Nova was something I relished doing occasionally on the weekends. With a warm sun shining down on the world, I'd roll down the windows and head anywhere the country roads were willing to take me. After a couple of hours of mindless driving, I'd head for home.

During warm weather, the snakes would crawl up from the canals and creeks and warm themselves on the roads and bridges. I almost always accidentally ran over the poor creatures, thinking they were just twigs or branches. I'd feel the bump and look in the rearview mirror in time to see the limp form rolling around. Even though my car outweighed the snake by a couple of tons, the bump was enough to cause me to go into a panic attack. I'd hold my breath for what seemed like forever, and the usual prickly skin feeling washed over me.

After I pulled into the driveway, shaking, I'd sit in the car for several minutes. I'd envision the poisonous snake, or its ghost, had wrapped itself around the driveshaft of my car, waiting for me to exit, when it would lash out at me, sinking its fangs into my legs. That would teach me for running over the sleeping reptile.

I may not have made it to Ireland, but I did move to the Evergreen State. We share space with approximately twelve species of snakes. Most of the snakes that thrive here are relatively harmless and live near the Columbia River Gorge. There are a few garter snakes found mostly in wooded areas, and near streams or ponds up and down the Puget Sound Region. Eastern Washington is home to the western rattlesnake, but that's hundreds of miles from where I reside. Until I'm whisked away to the Emerald Isle, I'm satisfied knowing that I won't be stepping on any pit vipers any time soon.

THE ITSY BITSY SPIDER

Craig Cook

Spiders are amazing creatures, are they not? The large, complex, beautiful webs they weave. Their role in making sure the world is not overrun with insects. Their variety of shapes and colors. Remarkable, really.

And I am terrified of them. Completely, absolutely, "run away screaming like a little schoolgirl" terrified. It doesn't matter if it's a large, hairy tarantula, or if it's some itsy bitsy thing smaller than the ball of my pinky finger. There is something undeniably repulsive about all arachnids in my mind.

When did this phobia, this paralyzing fear, manifest itself to me? I can't say for sure, although I know it was during my early childhood. I never saw *Arachnophobia* or any other spider-based film as a kid, so that wasn't it. I've simply been scared of them for as long as I can remember. The odd part about it is that I don't mind any other sort of insect, although I suppose spiders are not technically insects. The giant centipedes or lightning-quick silverfish that freak my wife out don't bother me. Just spiders.

I've always assumed it had something to do with learning early on in my life that by living in Kansas City, I would undoubtedly encounter both black widows and brown recluses, two of the most poisonous arachnids on the planet. Something about knowing these little things could do some serious, or possibly deadly damage if they ever bit me, made me grow paranoid. I looked everywhere before going under doorways, into closets, and especially to the garage.

My most memorable encounter with this disgusting species as a child was the summer I first started mowing the lawn. I don't remember my exact age, but that summer was a particularly nasty one for spiders. Every time I walked around the house, the corners where the gutters hung would, without fail, be housing a spider. And the ones hanging suspended in their webs that summer weren't little. I couldn't name the exact type of spider they were, nor do I have any desire to research the subject.

What I do know is that they were always light brown with a reddish tint mixed in, and they had these bulbous, grotesque abdomens that were roughly the size my adult big toe now is. There were typically five or six of these things hanging in various areas all around the house, and I refused to even consider mowing under them while they were alive. It didn't matter that they were always stationary, uninterested in me, and even if they were, couldn't descend quickly enough to touch me as I passed underneath. No, I refused to mow until they were dead. All of them.

So, on days when I had to mow, I always exited the garage with two things: a can of bug spray and a large broom (more on the broom in a bit). Now, I know what you're thinking. *Craig, if you have such a terrible phobia of spiders, how are you able to go hunt them down? Your fear must not be that bad.* But believe me, it was. However, many times my dad would be gone on mornings when I mowed, and my mom didn't see the point in killing anything that wasn't bothering her. Quite frankly, I was on my own, and my options were either walk under the creatures over and over, or find a way to dispatch them. I chose the latter. Not mowing because there were spiders outside seemed logical to me, but I knew it wouldn't go over with my parents.

I traveled from web to web, standing as far away as I could while still managing to hit the spiders with my bug spray. Coated with white foam, they would start thrashing while simultaneously sliding down to the ground, hanging from a thin sliver of silk. Many times, the arachnids would give a last ditch effort and begin climbing back up. In those cases, I would blast them again with the spray. Once they were on the ground, unmoving, I would stretch my leg out and smash them with the toe of my shoe. Had they been alive and moving, I'm not sure I could have done this, but perhaps knowing they were already dead gave me courage.

Once this task was done, I made my way to the back of the house, holding my broom, where the lawnmower and weed eater were kept in a storage shed. The door opening into the shed was the same style as a garage door, and in the corners, there would always be spiders. Not the large, bulbous kind that I found around the house, but smaller things, usually black. Standing far back of the door, I swept all around the corners until the path was clear. Then, once I'd opened the door, I had to sweep the inside area as well, for there were always a few more of the nasty things hiding inside.

This time-consuming task was bad enough, but what truly scarred me was what happened one summer day, while I was in the process of actually mowing. Believing I had eliminated any threat of attack, I was pushing the mower along the side of the house. I had never considered a spider might be hiding in the tiny little gap where the concrete foundation met the wooden siding of the house. I first noticed only a glimpse of movement out of the corner of my eye, but gasped loudly when I turned my head and saw what it was. Apparently startled by my commotion, one of the brownish-red spiders with the bulbous abdomens popped out from this little gap about an inch away from my left hand. I instinctively jerked away from it, letting go of the lawnmower and falling to my butt in the grass. It scuttled a little ways, then popped back into its hiding spot. The mower, meanwhile, rolled forward a little farther as the engine coughed and died.

I immediately vetoed using the mower along the side of the house as an option, as I could no longer see where the spider was. Instead, I retrieved the weed eater and completed the task by standing as far back as possible and stretching out to trim along the house.

Even now, years later, that day is forever burned into my memory, and I shudder when recollecting it. Over the years, I've endured much ribbing at the expense of my fear. Jokes from my parents and wife about freaking out by the sight of an itsy bitsy ol' spider. Members of a message board that I frequent, for both writers and readers of horror fiction, tease me relentlessly. Posting pictures of all sorts of arachnids, typically the biggest, ugliest, and flat-out freakish species they can find is a common occurrence. Any time I see a thread titled, "Hey, Craig!" I will almost assuredly get a glimpse of some disgusting surprise.

Yet perhaps the most disturbing example of what I've dealt with on a daily basis is from my young daughter. Out of nowhere one day, she came up with this wonderful game where she sticks her hand (or hands) out and wiggles her fingers. As she slowly advances toward me, she'll say, "The Emma spider is coming to get the big daddy spider. It's going to bite you."

She'll latch her hand around one of my fingers and make a *krrtch!* sound, which informs me I've been bitten.

Did my young daughter discover my phobia and decide to tease me about it, like everyone else? Or is this some kind of cruel, cosmic joke that everyone plays a part in? I can't even begin to imagine where she came up with such a horrendous game at age three.

But in addition to her bizarre game of playing spider, my daughter is also my source of hope when it comes to confronting my fears. When either my wife Kellie or I find a spider, I admittedly make her kill it; I can't do such a thing with Emma. Nor would I want to. Because, as strong as my fear of spiders can be, my fatherly instinct to protect my daughter is far more powerful.

Recently, Emma was playing in Kellie's and my room, shortly before her bath time. Standing and watching her, a small blotch above me caught my eye. It took me a moment to focus on what it was, as it was on the opposite side of the room. There, sitting still as could be on the ceiling, was a spider. Not a big one, about the size of a nickel, but enough to make me freeze and stare at it.

Emma noticed my distracted state and said, "What is it, Daddy?"

"It's a spider," I replied, and still I couldn't move. The stupid thing was in about as horrible a spot as I could imagine. First of all, it was on the ceiling, which meant I'd have to get under it to kill the creature. Secondly, it was above the bed, so while I could reach it easier, I would have to get much closer to it than I was comfortable with. Not to mention that if I simply succeeded in knocking it off the ceiling, the spider would fall on my bed. And, of course, it wasn't simply above any general part of the bed. It was directly above my pillow. For days afterward, I would think of that spider as I got ready for bed each night. What if there was another one? What if it waited until I was fast asleep in that pitch-black darkness, then decided to drop on my face? What if I woke up in the morning to my cheeks, eyes, and mouth all ballooned out from arachnid poison?

I knew I had to dispose of it. Kellie was at work, and Emma certainly couldn't do it. And leaving it up there wasn't an option, unless I wanted to sleep downstairs on the couch. Yet, I still had the problem of having it fall on my pillow, or in the blankets, or Heaven knew where else. Peeking into the bathroom, I saw a fairly large glass Kellie had left on the sink. Grabbing it, I returned to the bedroom. Emma kept asking me to get the spider, and I told her I would. I spotted a coaster on Kellie's dresser, and a plan formed in my mind.

Cautiously stepping onto the bed, still standing at a distance from the spider, I reached the glass out and put it up to the ceiling. Unfortunately, while the spider was trapped, it just sat there, upside down and stationary. I slowly slid the glass over, hoping to spook the thing into falling. I should have known better. Even after bumping it with the inside of the glass, the spider didn't move. I briefly wondered if it was dead, but found it hard to believe it would hold on upside down if it wasn't still living. After a couple more nudges, I managed to knock it off and slammed the coaster over the top of the glass. Still, it wasn't giving up. I don't know what it got its web attached to, but it caught itself and hung suspended in the air in the center of the glass. I shook it until the spider fell all the way to the bottom, hopped off the bed, and made a beeline for the bathroom.

Emma followed me with shouts of, "You got it, Daddy! You got the spider!"

Indeed I had, even if I was still a nervous wreck at that point. I opened the toilet lid, and sat the coaster on the sink. Like the unkillable villain in every horror movie ever made, the spider immediately made one last-ditch effort to foil my plan. As I looked back at the glass after setting the coaster down, I saw it climbing up the side of the glass in an effort to escape. I never knew until then that spiders could climb up glass.

I snatched the glass up and stuck it under the water faucet, filling it about a third of the way with hot water. As the spider thrashed around, I quickly poured all the contents into the toilet and flushed. The evil creature had been vanquished.

"Yay! Daddy, you got the spider!" Emma exclaimed while wrapping her arms around my leg in a hug. "You flushed it down the potty!"

I felt like I was her hero, the knight who had saved the damsel in distress from some horrific monster. It seems almost silly to think killing such a small creature would strengthen my strong belief in protecting my daughter from anything, but it did.

So, if I were to get into the business of helping others who suffer from arachnophobia (which won't happen), I could at least offer advice to the guys: have a daughter.

Sorry, ladies, but I don't know enough about your protective nature to speak for you. But I do know there are few things more powerful in this world than a father protecting his daughter, no matter how old she is.

And, guys, if you have a son instead? Well, at least you can get him to kill the spider for you.

The fact is, some things in life are more than worth the task of facing your worst fears head-on. Those things are few and far between, but they are there. For me, it's Emma. It may be something else for you—but if you have the opportunity, embrace it. And just be sure, when you flush that itsy bitsy spider down the toilet, it doesn't come climbing back up the waterspout.

FEAR OF THE MOVING STEPS

Shauna P. Norman

I had always believed that most people were only scared of elevators, or so I have been informed, but for me it always had been, and still is, escalators. I have now found, however, that this too is quite common and has been penned *escalaphobia,* of course.

I have absolutely no idea why or how this phobia developed. All I know is it is very real and, unlike other fears I have either overcome or learned to live with, e.g., frogs, I feel quite powerless over my fear of escalators.

I will recount for you some experiences that quite literally brought tears to my eyes (and possibly you to laughter) and in so doing, showed me that angels really are walking among us—disguised as humans.

For whatever reason, many of the country's worst escalators appear to pop up in railway stations and airports. By worst, I mean the biggest. They are so steep, long, high, seemingly never ending…call them whatever you like, they are big and I can feel my anxiety rising, just writing about them. That might be slightly exaggerated, but you get my meaning.

One of the most offending moving staircases I have ever had the displeasure of boarding was in an airport in New Zealand. I had had the best holiday you can imagine, seeing many of the wonders the country has to offer: the black sand at Muriwai; a cavity in what looks like the top of a mountain, but is actually an old inactive volcano; and the beautiful Rangitoto Island, which can sighted from numerous vantage points around Auckland, to name just a few.

I had apprehensively faced a perceived fear I felt I might have of flying, and surprisingly found I loved it so much that I have flown many, many times since, including in a four-seater with the only other person being a nineteen-year-old trainee pilot from Libya, because I wanted so much to see the breathtaking Hunter Valley from the air.

As my friend Damien and I entered the airport, I knew I looked every bit the contented tourist ready to return home from a beautiful holiday. But, then I spotted it: one of the most gigantic escalators I had ever seen in my life.

I grasped the black side rails. My knees shook and the palms of my hands dripped like a pashmina hung out to dry in the drizzling rain. We ascended at a seemingly painfully slow pace as perspiration oozed from the pores of my skin and dripped in smalls splashes onto my freshly ironed sweater. My makeup ran down my face so fast, I thought it had to be somewhere in a hurry. I was terrified.

A quarter of the way up, and I felt my stomach doing somersaults. Halfway up, and I felt like I was going to pass out; everything was spinning and my breathing had changed drastically. Three-quarters of the way up, and I felt myself falling backward. Thank goodness, Damien was behind me, because he caught me just as my legs began to give way. He made every gallant attempt to steady me, but in doing so, the inevitable domino effect took place and fellow travellers were thrown hilter-kilter and were grappling to right themselves. Even people up ahead of us, turning to see what the commotion behind them was all about, had their equilibrium thrown out of balance and thus became caught up in the mayhem. All I could hear were the echoing sounds of loud grunts, groans, and expletives.

By the time we reached the safety of a solid platform, I had a combination of relief and embarrassment coursing through me, and a desperate need to go to the ladies'.

I remember vividly another encounter with one of these feet-eating machines, when I aimlessly wandered into the Woolworths store located opposite Town Hall in George Street, Sydney. I made a couple of purchases, and if you have ever been in this particular store, you will know it is a peculiar maze of hot food facilities, grocery supplies, an underground subway, and much more. It really is an unusual layout, yet it seems to function well.

I spent a good half-hour there, and when I eventually attempted to leave, I found that the only way from where I was to where I wanted to be was to take an escalator down. I know, it made no sense to me, either. I froze. I mean it. I was like a rabbit caught in a glaring car light.

Tentatively, I approached two men standing behind a counter that was not really a counter. I asked them if there was an elevator I could use. One of the men quite unceremoniously told me no, it was out of order.

I asked, "What about steps?"

He again told me no.

I asked how I could go downstairs.

He snapped that I could use the escalator like other customers.

I stammered, "I can't."

His colleague obviously detected my distress and said, "Come with me."

I gingerly followed him to the staff service elevator.

Not only did this man travel right down to the subway with me in the slow old rickety elevator, but he entertained me with a story of his coming to Australia, how he got off the train at Town Hall, walked into Woolworths and asked for a job, and been ever there since. He told me it was a great job, and how he was studying to improve his English. I've never forgotten this young man from Pakistan. Not only had he recognized fear when he'd seen it, he'd acted to reduce it and bring about a sense of calm.

Another time, I was travelling by train to Sydney and had alighted at a major station. Commuters pushed and shoved as they mindlessly hurried and scurried to their respective destinations. I was propelled this way and that as I tried to fit into the running rhythm that they were all so used to. Finally, the crowd thinned enough for me to see that I was left with the back ends of many of them as they stood and even walked up the very steep moving steps.

I looked around for a stationary staircase, but could see none. To my left, I saw an elevator, with a state rail employee standing guard beside the foreboding barricade surrounding its doors. Now I was really scared. I warily approached the man and asked if there was another one I could use. He told me no and asked me, in broken English, why I did not take the escalator. I told him they scared me half to death. What he did next surprised me to no end. He removed the barricade and beckoned me into the elevator. I murmured something about it being broken, and as he ushered me into the open space, he then explained to me how people continually crammed themselves, to the point of hardly being able to breathe, into the station elevators rather than take an escalator or the stairs. He continued, in his broken English, that this was a strategy state rail occasionally adopted to help eliminate some of the overuse of elevators and encourage commuters to use the stairs and escalators.

As we moved fluidly along, he told me how his wife suffered with a chronic fear of elevators and so he fully understood my own reaction to the escalator. This, to me, was not a random act of kindness; it was a deliberate, kindhearted gesture from a compassionate heart.

Yet another incident involved, not a big escalator like the previous one, but actually quite a small one. However, the fear was just as real and just as debilitating in its own way.

I was having a lovely day out with some understanding friends who said encouraging words to help me as I boarded the steel jaw-like apparatus and felt the rise of the first step. Then, as usually is the way, the fear engulfed me. Suddenly, out of the blue, I heard this squeaky little birdlike voice beckoning me on.

There, above the stairs, stood a little old lady with her arms outstretched, telling me, "Come on, sweetie, you can do it, just hold on, it is going to be okay."

I might add, I was well into my forties at the time, but she was much older. There she stood like a guardian angel, waiting patiently until I reached the very top and then she put her hands out to help me off. She said something about it not being as bad as I thought and how brave I was. She too had recognized fear and, like a mother bird helping her chick on its first flight, she supported me through this experience.

Then there was the time I was rushing for an appointment and raced into a city building where I came face to face with, yes, you guessed it, another escalator. How many of these things are there? There I stood, rooted to the spot, full of both hesitation and apprehension, and out of the blue, two semi-cloned, better dressed, replicas of Miss Marple from Agatha Christie fame came rushing to my aid.

In no time at all, they found out what was wrong and while one politely grabbed hold of my handbag, the other took me by the elbow and guided me onto the escalator. They continued to be my shepherds, one standing beside me, continually holding my arm gently but firmly, whilst the other declared she was going to stand behind me to "provide a soft cushion" in case I fell. Once they deposited me safely on the level of my appointment and dutifully returned my handbag, they bustled off, holding onto each other and chattering away, happy with their lot.

I continued to stare after them in amazement for what seemed like an age. They had stunned me with their no-nonsense, yet sensitive, approach to my dilemma.

There are probably countless other escalator stories I could recount that simply don't come to mind at present, but these are some of the most memorable examples of not so much how my phobia affects me, but how, in doing so, it has affected others around me—usually complete strangers—and how, in all these cases (well, not so much in the first one), they befriended me and made light of the situation and even had a bit of a giggle.

You may wonder how this affects my family and friends. I will tell you, there are so many examples that I could not name them all. For example: all the times when we have walked across the whole length of a mall to find a staircase, across a complete city block to find an elevator, or even across a town to find an alternative venue rather than them put me through the anxiety of facing an escalator. My family, and especially Kathena, Brendan, Jack, and Yan, are especially sensitive to this phobia and never lose their patience, criticize me, or fail to explain if we are with a group why we are taking the long way. It has become almost second nature to us all to "walk the extra distance." And, let's face it, it is the healthier alternative.

How does it affect my day-to-day life? Fortunately, I usually live in rural-type locations that have very few, if any, escalators. When I go to the city now, I generally have a pretty good running knowledge of the major points to avoid. Like most people with any type of phobia, you learn if it can't be cured, how to work with it. I guess you could say, today I work with it to the best of my ability.

Rewriting this today, almost two years after it was first penned, I realize what a wonderful opportunity this phobia has given me to see compassion in action and how it has provided complete strangers the opportunity to reach out and be of service to a fellow traveler.

Mine is not to question why, and I suppose I could seek counseling on the matter, but then, I wouldn't want to miss out on some wonderful adventures and stories to tell.

THE MONKEY QUEEN

Emerian Rich

As a little girl, I had this reoccurring nightmare. Everything started nice and innocent. I was on a tropical island at a big luau. The dream was extremely vivid and in color, which was rare for me. A volcano in the distance spewed pink ash into the bright blue sky. The jungles were vibrant with life and color. Happy calypso music played in the background. All in attendance cheered as I was carried on a throne of bamboo and deposited at the head of a bedecked table. Dressed in a Hawaiian frock of loud oranges and greens, I sported a banana leaf skirt and flowers around my neck. Atop my head was a wreath woven from vines and hibiscus flowers. I was fanned by palm fronds and hundreds of exotic fruits were paraded before me.

I remember the taste of the mangos, grapes, kiwi, bananas, and papaya. The smell of the tropical flowers and fruits lulled me into a false sense of peaceful tranquility. Cool ocean air wafted over me, as if Mother Nature had found my perfect temperature and set the island's thermostat to please me. In a word, it was paradise.

I was the only human there, but that didn't bother me, because I was amongst friends. Snakes massaged my toes as they slithered past. Panthers and tigers yawned as they lay in the late afternoon sun. Macaws and toucans sang gleefully along with the drums beaten by tree frogs in tiki masks.

And then there were monkeys. Hundreds of the primates sat at my table and ate fruit, chattering happily as they paid homage to me, their ruler.

Little groups of two or three monkeys danced before me, putting on a show. They spun and twirled and did death-defying trapeze stunts. Several would come up at a time to honor me, or kiss my feet, or mist me with fragrant water. Some even sang or played musical instruments.

As the sun went down, torches were lit and the festivities got more rambunctious. Soon, the merriment became too much for me. The crowd got rowdy and I closed my eyes, thinking I might pass out from exhaustion. It was eight o'clock and I knew I had to get home before my curfew.

As I stood, the music stopped and all the monkeys turned to me. Hundreds of little beady eyes stared; their tails curled upwards into question marks.

They asked a flurry of questions.

"What can we get you?"

"Are you well?"

"Do you need something to eat or drink?"

"Where are you going, my queen?"

I smiled and patted the one closest to me on the shoulder as I said, "It's been lovely playing with you all, but now I must go home."

The monkey put his tiny fingers on mine and said, "Oh no, you are our queen. You can never go home."

I laughed at first, thinking he was joking, but as his fingers tightened on mine, I realized he was serious. Panic filled my heart and I screamed. I jumped down from my royal perch to the damp jungle floor. I ran as fast as I could through the dark jungle, trying to find my way home. I felt like Alice, running from all the cards. Vines tangled in my hair and lashed across my bare arms and legs as if trying to hold me back. I heard chattering and scampering of thousands of little monkeys chasing after me. The path never seemed to get clearer and as I looked around, I saw the menacing stares of red beady eyes at varying levels on trees, vines, and bushes. Every once in a while, I'd feel a scratch on my shoulder or a tickle on my ankles and I could never find my way home.

With the touch of a whiskery kiss at my neck, visions of being pulled apart by miniscule monkey nails shook me awake. My screams brought Mom. I recounted the tale between labored breaths as my adolescent heart raced and tears blurred my eyes. She assured me that no monkeys were or would ever be in the house. Glancing around the room, I would spot several places they could squeeze in. Through the ripped screen on the open window, under the closet door, or from the heater vent leading to the basement. I knew the creatures would invade my home. No matter how harmless or accommodating monkeys seemed, they were out for blood.

I don't know why I had these dreams. They were so real, they seemed like memories, not simply nightmares. Could they be a product of watching *Jungle Book* as a child? Were they past life memories or perhaps…a premonition?

As I grew up, my childhood nightmare blossomed into a full-blown phobia. Cute "Hang in There" posters on office walls featuring a monkey can conjure all kinds of horror stories in my mind. They are everywhere! Waiting to pluck out your eyeballs and juggle them for tips.

If you haven't been terrorized by a hoard of primates chasing you through a jungle, you probably don't realize just how many damned monkeys are around us every day. Curious George, Bubbles, *Planet of the Apes,* Barrel of Monkeys, Donkey Kong, Chunky Monkey, monkey bread, sock monkeys, marmosets, orangutans, baboons, the list just doesn't end! And don't even get me started on those friggin' cymbal clacking organ grinders.

When I hear in the news that some lady's face was ripped off by a monkey, I'm not shocked. Did you ever see that movie *Monkey Shines,* where a shoulder monkey terrorizes a man in a wheelchair? It should be turned into a public service film. I say, anyone who wants to own a monkey must watch this movie before adopting, because the things are evil, people!

I've tried to get over my primate aversion, but I just can't do it. Photos of the creatures make me shiver. While other people fear typing a word in on Google and having porn or blasphemous content pop up, I panic about the possibility of seeing one of those fanged mouths open in what some would say a laugh, but I say an evil shriek. I wait in fear of the day they will attack, tiny nails digging into my skin, creating infested blotches all over my body. Have you seen the pygmy marmosets that are so small, they wrap themselves around your finger? My skin crawls at the thought of their little bodies embedding themselves under my skin. Chilling!

Despite my distaste for primates, one of them has infiltrated my monkey-proof armor. Being an alternative lifestyle, child of darkness city dweller, people don't normally give me things that might have monkeys on them. *Nightmare Before Christmas* décor, spiders, and jack-o-lantern gifts abound, but primate nonsense? Not a whisper. I enjoyed this fact until I became pregnant with my son. Suddenly, all sorts of cutesy baby gifts poured in, many of them monkey themed. Most of them went straight to the giveaway pile, but there was one soft, fuzzy blanket I fell in love with by touch before I realized its sinister side. When my fingertips found the blanket at the bottom of a pink polka-dot box, it felt like wisps of cloud from heaven. I held the blanket to my cheek for fully five minutes, breathing in the deep scent of baby lotion, before my husband said, "Um, did you notice it has a monkey on it?"

Fear pierced my chest. I started breathing heavily and felt a tingle up my spine, as if I were being watched. My first instinct was to throw the evil blanket across the room—to distance myself from such a vile, ghastly object—but the touch of the baby-soft fabric made me hesitate. Was I being too judgmental, to chastise an item of such sensory enjoyment just because some manufacturer had wrongly decided to decorate it with the image of my nemesis?

I ultimately put the blanket in the keep pile, somehow knowing my newborn child would adore it. As predicted, it's become my son's favorite blankie. Since his birth, I've had to endure hundreds of movies containing monkeys. I keep my head turned, eyes focused on something else, praying not to hear the shrill monkey squeals from my dreams. If I happen to miss the appearance of one of these creatures on the screen, my son will point and squeal with delight, "Momma don't like monkeys!"

You would think my son's innocent delight in the vile creatures would make them more acceptable in my eyes. That with every trek through the zoo or watching of a primate cartoon, it would get easier to see them, easier to push my fear in the background. No such luck. I'm still just as much a *pithikosophobian* as ever.

I guess you could say a smidgen of the fear has gone, but is tolerance the same as acceptance? I don't think so. I still get nervous when people start talking about marmosets or pretend to be a monkey as they hand me a banana. And every time I wash that blanket, I wonder if the monkey is mocking me. Perhaps one day, the little bugger will peel himself from the plush fleece and hop onto my shoulder, pledging his undying love and pulling at my hair 'til I scream. He may even take me back to Monkey Island.

But for now, the blanket can stay, as long as it behaves, keeps my son happy, and doesn't sprout miniature fingers.

HONEY ARE YOU OK?

Anonymous

Mind at rest, lazy, easy,

Fourth of July home for two weeks

Sweet release from the desert heat

Drive the family over a long ride

Didn't see fireworks fall on their side

Explosion dead ahead in the road

Tracers come from the left adobe home

Caught without armor a nightmare unfolds

"Return fire" to the troops I scold

Suppress the ambush then count the loss

Hope no more grenades are tossed

The blinker turned to indicate fire from the left

What is taking so long for fire to suppress?

Look to the soldier in the other seat,

She, "Honey are you OK?" so sweet

My wife and my kids wonder what's wrong

It's a world far away a rest two weeks long.

Find a way to make it right.

Wife now drives on firework nights.

Returning home from a one-year tour

Sometimes takes years to endure.

Since that night, anxiety eased

With family happy and greatly pleased

So now on the Fourth, she takes the keys to drive

Everyday home to smiles I happily arrive.

THERE IS NO NEED

Denise Dumars

No being on this Earth needs more than six legs. H. P. Lovecraft made a career out of his fear of those with more; in his case, cephalopods, the eight-armed octopus and the ten-armed squid, both of whom may well inherit the Earth some day.

But not today. And I'm not afraid of them, in any case.

I am afraid of spiders. It's almost a joke—a horror writer afraid of spiders. Please, spare me. Yet there you have it. I have *arachnophobia*.

When I was in grad school, a psychology professor who had an office on the same floor as we English majors did said he could cure me of my phobia. The idea was to desensitize me, a little at a time. It made good sense. After all, I had done the same thing myself when my high school biology teacher had my lab partner and me sit on the side of the room closest to the tarantula cage.

I didn't want to be desensitized. A fear of spiders is a good thing. They are all venomous; some of them, including a few that are quite common here in California, can be deadly. Their neurotoxins can cause suffocation and death, or at the very least, severe pain, and sometimes even tissue necrosis. I cannot imagine a more frightening phrase than "tissue necrosis."

In any case, on a trip to Wrightwood for a writer's retreat, my fellow horror poets and I ran across a large black widow spider hanging from the handrail of the local bakery where everyone was lining up to buy coffee and rolls on a cold Saturday morning. What to do? What to do?

"Watch out for the black widow spider," I said to people who were about to grab the handrail. I sure wasn't about to go near it.

My mother told me that when she was cutting grapes for a living in California's San Joaquin Valley, she had seen a man who had been bitten by a black widow. The spiders were very fond of the dry grape arbors, apparently. She told me the man had to be taken to the hospital in the bed of a pickup truck because his convulsions were so bad that they couldn't get him into the cab.

I have never had to cut grapes for a living, but when I was teaching night classes at Los Angeles Harbor College, years before they remodeled our building, I held office hours before class. The shared office was very small and very dirty. My legs are also very long, so when I sat at the computer desk, I stretched them out beneath it. Sometimes, my ankles would bear interesting bites. Some were fleas, I hope; the others, I'm quite sure, were from spiders.

One hot summer night, I went to join friends at Ante's, a popular restaurant in San Pedro. I was wearing sandals without socks, and I have a rather painful bad foot. Later that night, when I was at home, my ankle started to itch, so I pulled up my pant leg to check it out. To my surprise and horror, two very large, red bites were on my ankle, about two inches apart. Then I noticed something interesting. The bites were above my bad foot and, until the bites healed, I couldn't feel any pain in it.

I was reminded of the people who let bees sting them because they say it lessens their arthritis pain. I have even heard people in Mexico say they let scorpions sting them for the same reason.

I have been stung by a bee only once. It was amazingly painful. A friend drew out the stinger with some tobacco from a borrowed cigarette. It continued to sting for a long time afterward. I have never actually *felt* a spider bite me, as I felt that bee sting me, but I'm not willingly going to let spiders bite me for any reason.

Do spiders have a natural anesthetic in their venom that prevents us from feeling the bite when it is given? Is that why we feel it only later? How long did it take for the man who was bitten by the black widow spider to start having convulsions?

Plus, I cannot stand the way spiders look. To me, they are hideously ugly. Of course, so are a lot of things and I'm not phobic about them! There's just something *wrong* about the way a spider moves, like it is not from this Earth. Maybe it isn't.

It takes a really big, thick magazine, such as *Travel & Leisure,* to kill a spider. You can spray them all day with hairspray, Lysol, or any other thing that would eventually suffocate a human, and the spiders just laugh at you. If you step on them and the soles of your shoes aren't hard enough, they'll get up and walk away. Can you imagine, proportionally, if someone of the same size ratio stepped on one of us? We'd be red jelly.

They are incredibly hard to drown, too, so don't flush them down the toilet unless you're absolutely sure they're truly dead before you do so.

I don't always kill spiders though. Sometimes I just ask them to go away, and tell them that if they don't, they will be killed. This quite often works, believe it or not.

I am not afraid of the following: giant flying cockroaches, like they have in New Orleans; rats and mice; alligators; rattlesnakes (within reason, of course); paper wasps, mud daubers, and yellow jackets; Gila monsters; or blood. I'm not usually afraid of snakes in general, unless they are at least as big around as my thigh.

I am afraid of crocodiles and feral hogs, however, because they both have a taste for "long pig."

I am not afraid of the desert or the ocean. I am afraid of the swamp and the woods. I like to see where I'm going.

There is no need to "cure" arachnophobia. It is a normal type of reaction to a deadly menace that can kill a grown man, unseen. A spider is not a natural type of creature. They are good for the environment, you might say. Yes, and arsenic is good for the environment in that it could kill off all humans, too, but I don't advocate that any more than I advocate allowing spiders to share living space with me.

I read some Freudian bullshit about how a fear of spiders is somehow a symbol for a fear of something sexual, specifically a woman's genitals (we assume this means the unshaven variety). Clearly, that diagnosis was aimed at men, but why? A raven is nothing like a writing desk, no matter what they say. The psych book didn't mention anything about why a woman might be afraid of spiders. Frankly, I don't think I really want to know.

However, it does interest me to find I am not the only horror writer I've met who is afraid of spiders. Even some famous horror writers have arachnophobia. Again, why? We're so good at scaring other people. We're unafraid of many things that we probably *should* be afraid of. So why are we scared of spiders?

But back to H. P. Lovecraft and his utter revulsion at seafood in general and the tentacled variety, in particular. I mentioned the Humboldt squid to one of my students who likes to go surfing up by Santa Cruz.

"Those things are disgusting!" he said, practically shuddering at the memory.

I had just seen a scientist on TV who believes that these squids are "our resident aliens" and described them as being nothing like any being that lives on dry land, or even like most other creatures of the sea. The scientist also said that because of global warming and the overfishing of the Humboldt squids' normal territory, the squid is now much more widespread than it ever has been before, and has even been known to nibble on human beings when its usual food sources get low. Maybe Lovecraft was onto something in being grossed out by these things. Just thinking of spiders gives me the willies, a feeling more akin to horror and revulsion than to fear.

Almost getting in a car wreck provokes the feelings of fear; the fear of spiders is something else altogether, an unreasoning, irrational terror that can literally drive a person mad.

For example, I bought a second-hand book on fairies when I was doing some research for an article. It was a really good book. I had set it on the arm of the sofa and had gone into another room for a time. When I got back to the sofa, there was a spider sitting on top of the book, the likes of which I have never seen in my home or, in fact, anywhere in California. It was grey and furry and stood rather tall and two of its eyes were looking right at me. I smashed it onto the cover of the fairy book and threw the book away and took the trash it was in out to the Dumpster immediately.

Just remembering it gives me a feeling that is akin to how I imagine I would feel if a psycho killer was coming toward me with a machete.

Sometimes, I think there is something wrong with me. My only comfort is in knowing that I am not alone. Surely, if enough people have this phobia that it has garnered a specific name in the annals of psychology, then there must be a good reason for it.

Somewhere, there is a photo of me at the Key Club in Hollywood in which tentacles are coming out of my mouth. I had just sent back an undrinkable martini and some calamari had been served. Many Lovecraft fans are fond of the eight- and ten-legged monstrosities that he feared.

I'll bet not many of them are fond of spiders. A program on one of those nature channels theorized that squids will inherit the earth, and I don't really have a problem with that. I just hope that if there is a God, he or she will not allow the spiders to do so.

There is no need to cure arachnophobia. Surely, evolution has imparted to at least some of us this "phobia" as a survival instinct for good reason.

ABOUT OUR WRITERS

Anonymous has written an extremely personal poem about an actual life event, and because the soul is bared and the event is searingly accurate, wishes to remain unnamed, but also wanted to share the uplifting outcome.

Kay Brooks is an author of three novels. *Disturbance* is self-published via Amazon Kindle. *Purgatory* and *Visions* have been taken on by publishing companies and are being prepared for release into the world of readers. Kay has also found time, in between running around after two perfectly boisterous boys, teaching English to secondary school pupils, and running away from mannequins, to write several short stories that have been published by Scarlett River Press.

Craig Cook is an aspiring author living in the suburbs of Kansas City with his wife and two children. He has a bachelor's degree in English: Creative Writing, as well as a minor in writing. He has worked as a copyeditor, page designer, and freelance reporter for the *Kansas City Star.* In his free time, he enjoys climbing mountains above 14,000 feet in Colorado. Currently, Craig has climbed 11 of Colorado's 58 "14ers." He can verify there are indeed spiders at 14,000 feet, and they terrify him up there far more than the height does.

Geoffery Crescent is a writer, editor, poet, and reviewer currently living in Bristol, England. In real life she's also an archaeologist, Ancient Hebrew fan girl, armchair Tolkienologist, and meat substitute product enthusiast. Her work appears in a variety of short story and poetry anthologies, magazines, and academic journals. She has also contributed to cookbooks, essay collections, and written and storyboarded an iPad app for children's comics. She's currently working on her first fantasy novel, as well as editing for independent comics, reviewing for various nefarious (and some not so nefarious) people and stalking the tattered streets of South West England performing what some have dubiously labelled as poetry. She also runs a blog where she suggests things to cook with meat substitute products.

Kim Curley's novella *Faith* can be found in the sci-fi/apocalypse anthology *Earth's End,* published by Wicked East Press in January 2012. Kim's first non-fiction piece, *Much Better, Thank You,* was included in the Hidden Thoughts Press anthology *Anxiety Disorders: True Stories of Survival,* published in April 2012. Although fiction writing is her passion, Kim is happy to share her personal stories through Hidden Thoughts Press so that "Other people don't have to feel alone!" You can find Kim online at: http://cupcakesblogcorner.blogspot.com; http://www.facebook.com/kim.curley1; and http://twitter.com/kim_curley.

Alyn Day is an active member of the New England Horror Writers, and lives outside of Boston, MA. She is an aid horror enthusiast with an inclination toward zombies. Publications include *So Long and Thanks for All the Brains; Daily Frights 2012; Women of the Living Dead; Zombie Tales; Here Be Clowns; Horror on the Installment Plan; Quick Bites of Flesh; Zombies for a Cure;* and the upcoming *Daily Frights 2013.*

Denise Dumars is a widely published author of poetry, short fiction, and nonfiction. Her most current book is *Preternatural Romance: Poems Romancing the Preternatural,* from Sam's Dot Press, 2012. She has just finished a novel and has a new nonfiction book and short fiction collection in process. She lives in the Los Angeles area, but her heart is in New Orleans.

J.T. Evans arrived on this planet and developed into an adult in the desolate, desert-dominated oil fields of West Texas. After a year in San Antonio, he spent a year in the northern tundra of Montana. This yearlong stint prepared him for the cold (yet mild, compared to Montana) climate of the Front Range of Colorado. He has thrived in the Mountain State since 1998 with his lovely Montana-native wife and newly created son. He primarily pays the bills by performing software engineering and other technocentric duties.

Shauna Klein is a freelance writer, website designer, and overall Jill Of All Trades who lives in sunny/stormy Florida. Shauna Klein is her pen name and she is married with children that have fins, feathers, and fur. She is an affiliate member of the Horror Writers Association. She has a short story in the *Cemetery Dance* book, "In Laymon's Terms," and a blurb in the book *The Ice Limit* by Douglas Preston/Lincoln Child. She has been published in *Death Head Grin* and will be published in *Grave Demand Magazine.* You can find a review of "Peaceable Kingdom" on *Schlock Magazine,* as well as her short stories on Amazon through Prairie Rose Press. Look for more short stories to come and later, a book on *The Twins of Terror,* a book for children about two tenacious Belgian Malinois brothers who always find trouble. Facebook: http://www.facebook.com/authorsklein. Website: http://shaunaklein.com.

Shauna P. Norman grew up in the tiny town of Corindi Beach in NSW, Australia, and knew early that she wanted to write. It is only more recently that she embraced the road to publication; although she has had poetry and several personal short stories in minor publications, she is only now taking it seriously. Shauna has spent the past few years sifting through old manuscripts, a poetry portfolio, and numerous short stories, whilst further improving her writing skills and now finally feels it is time to step onto the road of her next adventure. To learn more about Shauna, visit https://www.facebook.com/ShaunaPNorman

Angie Orenstein lives in Billerica MA with her husband, Aaron, and her teenage daughter Adria, who shares her mother's love of writing. Angie is a writer for her hometown newspaper. She grew up in Hudson, NH with her mother, father, and younger sister. She graduated from Notre Dame College in Manchester, NH with a BA in Communications, then worked in an advertising department of a newspaper. Her hobbies include reading—some of her favorite authors are James Patterson, Dean Koontz, and Jodi Picoult—and she likes to go jogging and take aerobics and Zumba classes.

David Price lives in Peabody, Massachusetts. David has worked as a hardwood floor contractor for more than twenty-five years. His dream is to be a full-time writer.

Emerian Rich is a writer, artist, and Horror Hostess of the popular international podcast *HorrorAddicts.net*. She is the author of the *Night's Knights* Vampire Series and also writes the *Sweet Dreams Musical Romance* series under the name Emmy Z. Madrigal. For more information about Emz, visit emzbox.com.

Suzanne Robb is the author of *Z-Boat*, coming in March 2014 from Permuted Press; *Were-wolves, Apocalypses, and Genetic Mutation, Oh My!* from Dark Continents Publishing; and *Contaminated: A Zombie Novel*, from Severed Press. She is a co-editor of *Anxiety Disorders – True Stories of Survival*, Hidden Thoughts Press, and, with Adrian Chamberlin, of *Read the End First*, Wicked East Press, which made the Stoker Recommended Reading List, 2012. In her free time, she reads, watches movies, plays with her dog, and enjoys chocolate and LEGOs.

Janet Scott-Buckley: From an early age, Janet enjoyed reading and writing, and focused on those throughout college, where she took literature courses and was a Teaching Assistant in a writing course for Psychology majors. Janet graduated from the University of Massachusetts at Amherst with a Bachelor of Science degree in Psychology, and a minor in Women's Studies. Janet obtained a Master's Degree in Clinical Social Work, with a Certificate in Family Therapy from Boston University, after which she worked as an outreach clinician with children and families in urban areas north of Boston. Janet made a career change in 1995, and is now a manager and commercial lines specialist with a large insurance agency in Massachusetts. She also works with her husband Mark in their web design business, Buckley Web Design, writing and editing content for client web sites. *Eight Feet of Terror* is Janet's first published work.

Jay Sutter lives in the beautiful hills of western Massachusetts. He is a passionate substitute teacher for all subjects, including writing. A former letter carrier and intelligence reporter, Jay's unique experiential insights are presented in his writings. He contributed a short story under a pen name in a transgressive fiction book, *Writings on the Wall*, published in 2012. Current hobbies are photography, songwriting, hiking, and coffee. Jay is quite proud of his three awesomely creative children Cassandra, Adria, and Nate.

Toianna Wika is a freelance writer who lives in St. Paul, MN with her husband and two children. She has worked as a mental health technician, likes to share personal experience stories, and advocates on behalf of human rights.

ABOUT HIDDEN THOUGHTS PRESS

We are a publishing house dedicated to producing quality books about real people with real stories of coping with, and surviving, mental illness. We want to help individuals tell their stories, and offer them, their families, and their friends help, hope, and a place to share and encourage.

For more about us, see www.HiddenThoughtsPress.com, and view our books on Amazon.com and other retailer sites.

www.ingramcontent.com/pod-product-compliance
Lightning Source LLC
Chambersburg PA
CBHW071905020426
42331CB00010B/2681